THE FACE

SIX GREAT CLIMBING ADVENTURES

THE FACE

SIX GREAT CLIMBING ADVENTURES

Richard Else and Brian Hall

BBC BOOKS

SAFETY

Climbing can be a dangerous sport and should be practised only after the skills have been learnt, using the correct equipment. All the climbers described in this book are highly experienced, and many of the techniques they use are not recommended for the novice.

PICTURE CREDITS

BBC Books would like to thank the following for providing photographs and for permission to reproduce copyright material:
Dave Cuthbertson: pages 14, 38, 55, 66, 102–3; Mark Diggins: page 98; Richard Else: pages 3, 26, 35, 41, 50–1, 58–9, 63, 68, 74–5, 79, 82–3, 106, 126, 135, 146, 163, 174–5, 178–9, 183, 186, 194–5, 201; Brian Hall: pages 6, 18–9, 31, 34, 42, 47, 62, 70, 90, 95, 110, 115, 122–3, 127, 130, 138, 142–3, 151, 154, 158, 167, 170, 190, 198.

PAGE 3 Sabbah Atieeq leads Di Taylor and Tony Howard along the broad ridge to the summit of Jebel Rum in Wadi Rum, Jordan.

This book accompanies the television series *The Face: Six Great Climbing Adventures,* which was produced by Triple Echo Productions for BBC Scotland.
Executive Producer for the BBC: Colin Cameron
Series Producer/Director for Triple Echo Productions: Richard Else

Commisioning Editor: Nicky Copeland
Project Editor: Khadija Manjlai
Copy-editor: Hugh Morgan
Art Director: Linda Blakemore
Designer: Rachel Hardman Carter
Maps: Dave Cuthbertson
Glossary illustration: Alan Burton

ISBN 0 563 38319 4

First published in Great Britain in 1998
Published by BBC Books, BBC Worldwide Limited,
Woodlands, 80 Wood Lane, London W12 0TT

Set in Plantin Light and Franklin Gothic by BBC Books
Printed and bound in Great Britain by Butler and Tanner Limited,
Frome and London
Colour separations by Radstock Reproductions Limited, Midsomer Norton
Jacket printed by Lawrence Allen Limited, Weston-super-Mare

Contents

Acknowledgments

This book, and the television series that it complements, simply could not have been undertaken without the enthusiastic help and unflagging support of a large number of people. Firstly, our thanks should go to BBC Scotland and especially to Ken MacQuarrie, who originally commissioned the series, and to Colin Cameron, who brought his incisive editorial eye and enthusiasm to bear on the realization of the films. Their continuing commitment to this genre of programme-making, with its inherent difficulties, will be appreciated by all outdoor enthusiasts. Similarly, our thanks go to Neil Fraser for his advice and especially to Brenda Macarthur, without whose untiring support it would not have been possible to realize this project in the way we all wished. At BBC Books our thanks are due to editors Nicky Copeland and Khadija Manjlai; to copy-editor Hugh Morgan and to designers Linda Blakemore and Rachel Hardman Carter for once again coping with the demands and changing deadlines inevitable in any real adventure.

'On the hill', an ambitious project such as this relies on a whole-hearted commitment that is well above and beyond any call of duty. Therefore we particularly thank the film team of Duncan McCallum, Keith Partridge, Simon Ffrench and a safety team of James Blench, Dave Cuthbertson (who also skilfully drew the topos for this book), Mark Diggins, Grant Statham and John Whittle, together with our Canadian cook Sylvia Harron. Similarly, all our climbers hung in the most precarious of positions for both still and movie photography and then, instead of relaxing, had to recount their life histories for the benefit of this book. Put all of this into the most demanding of schedules and they clearly deserve a special vote of thanks.

In Jordan, the Ministry of Tourism provided most valuable assistance, as did Royal Jordanian Airlines. The traditional friendship, trust and a good deal of mischief came from Sabbah Atieeq, Sabbah Eid, Atieeq Auda and their fellow Bedouin of Wadi Rum. Our travel in Vietnam was immeasurably eased by Mr Tue of Hanoi Tours and the Ministry of Foreign Affairs. Our attention was first brought to the splendours of Ha Long Bay by Maria Coffey and Dag Goering whose help on location was invaluable. (Thanks too for preventing our land-loving chief safety officer from drifting off into the South China Sea.) In the USA Lorna Burgess offered us her traditional superb hospitality; Doug Heinrich and Nancy Feagin undertook valuable research and any trip with Aid Burgess to Moab must include a special thank you to the manager of Moab Brewery in the town. The initial visit to Pabbay would not have been possible without the research of Phil Swainson. We remember with affection Archie Campbell dropping us on the island and to Ivor Griffith of PDG Helicopters airlifting us off when the novelty of being stranded had begun to wear thin. During our filming there we once again enjoyed the superb company of Jamie and Marion Robinson of Doune Marine, Knoydart, and the luxury of their fine boat *Mary Doune*. Jim Broadbent and Jacques Harvey are expert bush pilots, and their determination not to let the weather upset our schedule in the Cirque of the Unclimbables was much appreciated, as was the assistance given by our old friends at Yamuska Guides in Canmore. The help given by Fort Simpson's tourism

Airlie Anderson starts the difficult second pitch of Primrose Dihedral, Moses Tower, Utah. Her hands are taped to protect them from the continuous crack climbing found on the route.

ACKNOWLEDGMENTS

officer, Clarence Villeneuve, is beyond any simple vote of thanks: without his help we would not have been able to accomplish even half of our plan. If you're passing through Fort Simpson say 'hi' to all three on our behalf and spend some time in Nahanni Inn's coffee-shop listening to the locals. Finally, our trip to South Africa was eased by André Schoon of the Mountain Club of South Africa, whose greeting of a weary team on arrival at Cape Town airport was an unexpected bonus. Douw Steyn was not only our runner but also provided valuable research, and the sheer driving enthusiasm of Ed February was vital to the whole enterprise.

Any manufacturer supplying equipment to us knows it will be used in the most difficult of situations, so special thanks are due to the following: DMM, Lowe Alpine, Mountain Equipment, The North Face (especially Stephen Jessey), Scarpa, Troll and Wild Country. Without their help, many of these climbs could not have been undertaken, and in all cases we can say honestly that their equipment performed extremely well in situations of both use and abuse! Similarly, without the help of Sony, who shipped pre-production versions of their new DVC professional cameras, the filming would not have been possible. We must also mention Phil Brown Production Consultants of Bristol and the superb service provided, as always, by the specialist Nikon dealers, Grays of Westminster, for understanding our special needs. Both companies remained calm in the face of very tight deadlines.

Finally, our special thanks go to Laura Hill and David Taylor at Triple Echo Productions who offered continuous support and encouragement throughout what was an incredibly ambitious undertaking that lasted a year and a half. Brian Hall would particularly like to thank Vanita Warden and his wife, Louise, for their incisive and valuable comments on the manuscript, while Richard Else acknowledges that without the myriad difficult jobs undertaken by Margaret Wicks neither the book nor the films would have come to fruition.

Our heartfelt thanks go to you all and we promise not to do it again – until the next time.

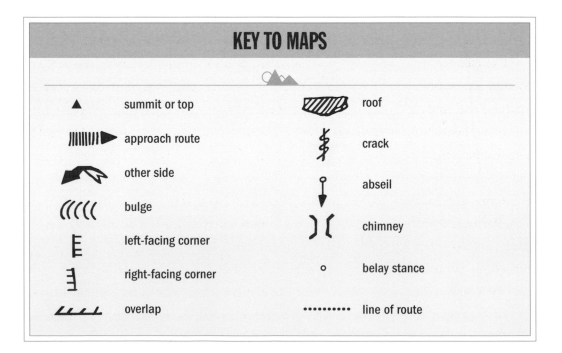

KEY TO MAPS

▲	summit or top		roof
	approach route		crack
	other side		abseil
	bulge		chimney
	left-facing corner	○	belay stance
	right-facing corner		
	overlap	··········	line of route

Introduction

'So why *exactly* do you do it?' That is a question climbers get used to being asked. Often it comes from people who view climbing as a macho death or glory activity pursued by the foolhardy and irresponsible. This feeling can be reinforced by newspaper articles that often do not place a high regard on accurate reporting and concentrate almost exclusively on accidents in high mountain environments.

Yet climbing has never been more popular or more varied than it is today, and while a number of people aspire to tackling demanding routes at altitude in some of the world's least hospitable places, many others search out sun-drenched rock in exotic locations or local crags just a short distance from where they live. What unites this diverse group of people is that they are undoubtedly highly motivated and usually very articulate. This book and the television films to which it is integrally linked have tried to reflect the richness and variety of today's climbing. The participants are not just the 'professionals' (in that they climb full-time and get most of their income from doing so) but are archaeologists, fine artists, writers, photographers, professional guides, company directors, and, in the case of Aid Burgess, a house-husband and amateur brewer.

The climbers encompass a huge range of concerns, including environmental and political issues, but all are passionate about the thrill of vertical ground. Some, like Joe Simpson and Andy Parkin, have suffered accidents that would deter lesser people from ever tying themselves on to a rope again. Airlie Anderson, Nancy Feagin and Lynn Hill demonstrate amply that the sport (if climbing can be described in that way) is not a male preserve and that women can achieve as much if not more than their male counterparts. Similarly Tony Howard and Di Taylor, who are partners on and off the rock, illustrate that the sheer fun that comes from climbing is not limited to the under-fifties and also that climbers can sometimes make incredibly close bonds with the indigenous population, sharing both their hopes and fears. Not since T. E. Lawrence over 70 years earlier have the Bedouin people held someone from Britain in such respect. Equally, not since Lawrence has anyone from outside so effectively championed the Bedouin cause. Finally, there is the sheer thrill of climbing at, or very near, your limit exemplified by Greg Child's pounding heartbeat and inventive vocabulary as he inched his way up Boat People, the new route in Vietnam's spectacular Ha Long Bay.

This book and the television films do not attempt to answer the 'why do you do it' question, partly because there are countless answers and partly because all answers can show only a section of a more complex picture. Rather, we wanted to see what drives 12 highly motivated individuals in a wide range of situations, from the opening up of new climbing areas to eavesdropping on the stresses that accompanied two outstanding practitioners – Lynn Hill and Dave Cuthbertson – as they attempted what they claimed was one of the hardest traditional rock-climbs in Britain. And although the world is a rapidly shrinking place, we wanted to show the excitement of travelling to some of the most exciting locations in search of great rock. There is the sense of real exploration in the desert of Wadi Rum in Jordan or the sheer unpredictability that accompanies any expedition to the Cirque of the Unclimbables in Canada's Northwest Territories which, by any standards, is one of the world's more remote landscapes. In Vietnam there are the challenges of dealing with a bureaucracy that, although rapidly changing, is unfamiliar with the idea that climbers actually *enjoy* finding their way up difficult overhanging rock and do so for pleasure.

Finally, at its best, climbing is about having fun with enjoyable companions, and while this is present in all the films, no one could have failed to have been moved by the black South African Ed February, who told us, in the most stark way, that even climbing was not exempt from the evil that embraced his country for so many years. His optimism for the future, while not forgetting the lessons of the past, is an inspiration to everyone. Which also makes it clear that climbing is not simply about just climbing.

From boulders to Everest

Climbers follow a style or set of ethics which can be loosely described as how they choose to climb. It is a handicap system that tries to maintain the challenge and degree of uncertainty of the ascent. The handicap disallows certain equipment and methods in one type of ascent, but allows them in other types of ascent. To take an extreme example: to use a ladder to get to the top of a short outcrop of rock would totally destroy the climbing challenge, but used to cross a crevasse in the Khumbu Icefall below Everest it is acceptable, as this one piece of aid does not tip the scales towards certain success. Generally, the use of equipment is a personal issue unless the rock is damaged permanently, such as when bolts are placed, when there are wider environmental questions. Additionally, the ethics of the first ascensionists often set a precedent for future ascents. To add to the confusion of the layman, there are no written rules.

In 1967 the American climber Lito Tejada-Flores wrote an influential article called 'Games Climbers Play' which explained logically the broad spectrum of the sport by dividing it into seven recognizable games. He wrote: 'Climbing is not a homogeneous sport but rather a collection of differing (though related) activities, each with its own adepts, distinctive terrain, problems and satisfactions, and, perhaps most important, its own rules'.

The bouldering game

This is the purest form of climbing (with the most rules) in which a climber tries a short sequence of moves near the ground, typically on a large boulder. It is solo climbing (without ropes) where technical aids are banned and the climber's strength and ability are what counts. Bouldering is generally only taken to a height where it is safe to jump off and is therefore relatively risk-free. It is regarded as one of the best ways of training for rock-climbing, and most indoor climbing walls have a 13-foot- (4-m-) high artificial bouldering wall. Bouldering is becoming an increasingly popular game in its own right, with many climbers specializing in this niche of the sport.

The crag-climbing game

Crags, outcrops and small cliffs are the home of the most popular game of climbing. The height of the cliff requires the use of ropes and equipment to protect against a potentially dangerous fall. Today the usual ethic is to try to free-climb naturally, using only handholds and footholds, whereas gaining help by pulling or resting on pitons, bolts or nuts is regarded as artificial-aid climbing and hence failure. The types of climbing gear used for protection sub-divide this game into two. Traditional (trad or adventure) climbing uses protection gear, such as nuts, cams or slings, placed by the lead climber which utilize the natural features of the rock, such as cracks or spikes. Because the opportunity to place this equipment varies with the nature of the rock, protection can be unpredictable and at irregular intervals, which makes traditional climbing more adventurous (and sometimes more dangerous) than the second type of crag-climbing, sport climbing. Here, pre-placed bolts at regular intervals are used as protection. This is often safer and takes the uncertainty out of protecting the climb, allowing the climber to concentrate on the actual climbing. Sport climbing is growing rapidly throughout the world, its safe, gymnastic excitement appealing equally to both men and women, and the skills involved soon mastered by the young. Indoor climbing walls and competition climbing use the methods and ethics of sport climbing. The climbing in the chapters on Pabbay, Vietnam and South Africa typify the crag-climbing game.

The continuous climbing game

This is played on bigger cliffs where time (up to a day) and other objective dangers such as weather may dictate the style of the climbing. In the name of speed the 'rules' are relaxed a little and artificial direct aid is used occasionally. More recently, as standards rise and ethics of ascents are keenly debated, the 'rules' of crag-climbing are being introduced into this game. Ascents of short ice and mixed (ice and rock) climbs come into this category though the equipment used would be very different and indicate yet another subdivision within the sport. The routes in Jordan and Utah are good examples of the continuous climbing game.

Big wall-climbing game

This game is played on the big rock walls of the world, typified by multi-day ascents of technically demanding routes that usually combine free-climbing and climbing with the use of aids. The climb can be made in one push, where the climbers bivouac overnight on the wall; a variation of this is a capsule ascent where fixed rope is used between suitable bivouac sites. One of the big challenges in climbing is to bring the crag-climbing ethic to this game and make one-day free ascents of these huge walls. The route described in the chapter on Proboscis in the Cirque of the Unclimbables is a big wall-climb in an alpine environment.

Alpine climbing game

Due to the objective dangers of storms, rock-fall, avalanche and variable snow conditions presented by the mountain environment, speed is essential in alpine climbing. This has led to the relaxation of what is considered acceptable practice. Free and aided rock-climbing combine with snow and ice techniques in an ascent where safety comes first and where greater merit is often placed on reaching the summit than on the style used in getting to it. Alpine-style climbing is traditionally a two-man ascent in which all the gear and food is carried by the climbers. Overnight bivouacs are sometimes necessary, and a full range of mountaineering skills is required by the party. One result of the all equipment being carried in rucksacks and the clothing worn for potentially hostile conditions is that the climber is restricted from performing at the same technical level as in the crag game.

Super-alpine climbing game

This is regarded as the most dangerous and committing of the climbing games. It is an extension of the alpine game but in serious and hostile mountains like those found in the greater ranges, such as the Peruvian Andes and the Himalayas, Arctic regions or the Alps in winter, where cold, altitude and remoteness all challenge the climber. The routes often take many days and are physically and mentally demanding. Just surviving is often hard enough! There are no constraints on using the full range of climbing techniques but the team must be self-contained and not use fixed rope.

The expedition game

This involves the conquest of large mountains by almost any means and there are few rules. By using big teams of climbers, fixed ropes, oxygen, high-altitude porters and a series of camps, the mountain is climbed over a long period of time. The argument is that the high mountains have sufficient defences to require no rules, and success will always be in doubt. Unfortunately, national interests, sponsors or media coverage are often given more importance than climbing ethics, and the mountain is frequently beaten into submission by the overuse of resources (sometimes even helicopters). The cost of such expeditions is astronomical and this is one of the reasons why most expeditions to mountains such as Everest are now commercially funded by fee-paying clients who want to be guided up the mountain. Many climbers regard expedition climbing as a dinosaur, as most mountains (including all the 26,250-foot/8000-m peaks) have been climbed in the super-alpine climbing game without oxygen.

Greg Child and Andy Parkin

Ha Long Bay, Vietnam

1

The kayak skimmed across the calm, green tropical water of the bay. Above towered the grossly overhanging ochre and grey limestone wall that Andy and Greg intended to climb. There was no landing place, so they positioned the kayak below a small shelf 15 feet (4½ m) above the sea from where they hoped to start the climb. With an ungainliness that threatened to tip the boat, Andy stood up and grabbed the wet, barnacle-encrusted rock that had been eroded into contorted razor-sharp honeycombs infested with small crabs. The action of the sea had undercut the pinnacle to such an extent that a concentrated effort and a couple of forceful pulls were needed before he established himself on the rock. Without the security of a rope and laden with all his climbing hardware, Andy was acutely aware that if he fell he would demolish the kayak, which would sink like a stone into the cloudy water below. With care he tested each hold before trusting his weight to the rock. Strenuously, he pulled on to the shelf. Greg followed. They could now start the serious climbing.

Sweating in the midday sun, Greg Child leads the second pitch of Tombstone Wall. He is struggling to place protection while Andy Parkin patiently belays on the hanging stance below.

Greg Child had arrived a few days earlier at Hanoi, where he became part of a snake of Western travellers queuing patiently for admission to the country. He had made his own circuitous way from Seattle, on the west coast of America, where he now lives. He had done better than Andy Parkin, who, attempting a difficult ice-climb above Chamonix, had been in the mountains for nearly 48 hours, then made a mad dash to Heathrow but had since somehow got lost in the mayhem of Hong Kong Airport and missed the final leg of the flight.

In common with virtually all other foreign travellers, one vital document was apparently missing and everyone followed the frantic gesturing of local officials to find a man with a Polaroid camera and a rubber stamp who, for the customary few dollars, completed the mysterious additional form. More frantic gesturing and the arrivals were let through immigration and out into the heat of Hanoi.

Hanoi is still a city where most people get around on bicycles, where the upwardly mobile display their status by riding appropriately named Honda Dream mopeds and where cars are still comparatively scarce. Here, extended family groups crowd the narrow streets, where they eat and live during the day, moving at night to tiny rooms above their shops. There is also an indomitable spirit which accepts that nothing is unachievable: you see, for example, the most improbable-looking loads being transported on the back of push-bikes. It soon becomes a competition to spot the most outrageous cargo, and sightings have included the moving of a settee, two pigs and a large quantity of house bricks!

In the Western world Hanoi is remembered as the capital of North Vietnam, when the country was divided into North and South Vietnam. In the war between the two countries, South Vietnam was supported by the United States and in the years between 1965 and 1973 the Vietnam War was reported daily in the world's press. It was a conflict that, at its height, saw over half a million US troops stationed in the country, together with smaller contingents from South Korea, Australia, Thailand and New Zealand.

For a whole generation, especially those with American links, names such as the Mekong Delta, Da Nang, the Tet Offensive and the Ho Chi Minh Trail will always remain indelibly etched in the memory. It was a conflict that left nearly 50,000 Americans dead and over 300,000 wounded, while about 250,000 South Vietnamese service people also lost their lives, with almost 600,000 wounded. In

North Vietnam about 900,000 troops were killed and around 2 million maimed. Hundreds of thousands of civilians on both sides suffered, with many killed as the result of US bombing; the countryside was scarred both by the bombs and defoliation, and the cities were heavily damaged. Industry, commerce and agriculture came to a standstill, and many people in the South became refugees seeking to escape from the fighting. It is said that there were an estimated 20 million bomb craters; that 800,000 children were orphaned (including those abandoned by GI fathers); that there were 2 million widows, and that in North Vietnam not a single bridge survived the American air raids. Even in a country where statistics are notoriously unreliable, this adds up to an appalling legacy.

But these events are now part of the country's turbulent history, with reunification declared in 1976. Today, although rapid economic development is beginning, the country still remains poor. For years it was blighted by an American-led embargo on aid, and only since 1986, with the introduction of *doi moi* (economic renovation) has the economy begun to develop, with inflation falling from 700 per cent in 1986 to around 14 per cent a decade later. Even so, the government still wrestles with the problems of accepting an economic free market within a Communist framework and of allowing its citizens the freedom to criticize the administration. Once stereotyped by war, the Vietnamese are friendly and incredibly industrious.

After a day to recover from their various journeys, Andy Parkin and Greg Child thankfully left the noise of Hanoi and its crowded, narrow markets (where you can examine dozens of varieties of fish, have poultry freshly killed on the spot and where literally every part of the animal is for sale) for the countryside. But here, where the economy is still predominantly agricultural, the landscape is as crowded and active as the city. The journey, in a smart Ministry of Tourism Mercedes air-conditioned bus, reflected the country's desire to encourage travellers with their important foreign currency. It is approximately 90 miles (154 km) from Hanoi to the coastal community of Bai Chay, which lies on Ha Long Bay.

Unloading fish and coal at Hon Gai market waterfront, Ha Long Bay. Offshore, some of the archipelago's 2000 limestone towers, which offer so much climbing potential.

Throughout its length the route was a scene of relentless activity, with groups of people building houses, and peasants laying out their rice crop to dry on their porches and gardens and, where these were insufficient, continuing on side roads and tracks. Water buffalo pulled crude ploughs in a ritual that is clearly unaltered in centuries, while occasionally two people could be seen irrigating fields by operating a water container slung in a wooden frame. Everything – pedestrians, cyclists, cattle and buffalo – shared the narrow road with a number of squat trucks whose two-stroke engines were of a primitive design.

Often the road was so noisy and crowded – near misses were common – it resembled an Old Testament exodus, and the tortuous five-hour journey left a variety of strong impressions, but nobody was prepared for the next stage – travelling through Ha Long Bay.

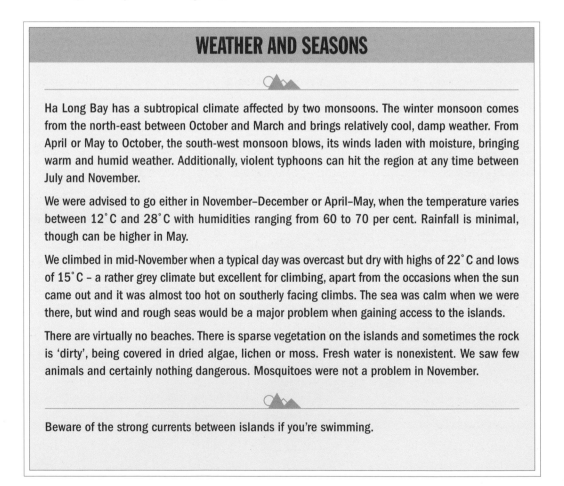

WEATHER AND SEASONS

Ha Long Bay has a subtropical climate affected by two monsoons. The winter monsoon comes from the north-east between October and March and brings relatively cool, damp weather. From April or May to October, the south-west monsoon blows, its winds laden with moisture, bringing warm and humid weather. Additionally, violent typhoons can hit the region at any time between July and November.

We were advised to go either in November–December or April–May, when the temperature varies between 12°C and 28°C with humidities ranging from 60 to 70 per cent. Rainfall is minimal, though can be higher in May.

We climbed in mid-November when a typical day was overcast but dry with highs of 22°C and lows of 15°C – a rather grey climate but excellent for climbing, apart from the occasions when the sun came out and it was almost too hot on southerly facing climbs. The sea was calm when we were there, but wind and rough seas would be a major problem when gaining access to the islands.

There are virtually no beaches. There is sparse vegetation on the islands and sometimes the rock is 'dirty', being covered in dried algae, lichen or moss. Fresh water is nonexistent. We saw few animals and certainly nothing dangerous. Mosquitoes were not a problem in November.

Beware of the strong currents between islands if you're swimming.

Over 3000 islands, limestone pinnacles and rock spires make up a maze that is regarded as one of the wonders of Asia, an area virtually untouched and unexplored by climbers, but one that has the potential to become one of the world's great rock-climbing venues. Each island is unique and many feature grottoes sculpted by the wind and waves. The waters around the islands are populated by 'boat people' or 'water gypsies', who live on primitive boats about 14 feet (4 m) long which are entirely open except for a crudely covered living space in the centre. Whole families live on these craft, making a living from fishing and often coming alongside tourist boats to sell their catch. Even when boats were moving at speed across the bay they would skilfully manoeuvre alongside and tie up to try to make a sale. At night the boats moored together in sheltered spots, making temporary floating villages illuminated by the flickering of dozens of gas lanterns and open cooking fires in their sterns.

Anthropologists would have had a field day researching how these people's lifestyle had originated; estimating their population and their income; and establishing how their society was organized, together with a hundred other questions. Greg and Andy were here, of course, for the climbing, and the fact that they were to undertake some demanding first ascents together was no accident.

Greg Child is one of the world's most accomplished climbers, with an impressive climbing record. Now 40, he has established new routes on Himalayan peaks, including Shivling, Gasherbrum IV and Trango Tower, together with successful ascents of K2, Broad Peak and Everest. Greg has also made numerous first ascents on rock walls in both his native Australia and his adopted United States. He is a seasoned traveller, and his climbing has taken him around the world from the Andes to Alaska. Recently, he visited the Ak-Su range in Kyrgyzstan (formerly part of the USSR), climbing in the company of such outstanding luminaries as Lynn Hill.

Yet Greg's climbing started almost by accident. He was brought up in the Sydney suburbs, where his father ran a small office supply company and his mother looked after the home. Child junior and senior had little in common and, like many teenagers and fathers, they did not get on well together.

Looking back some 30 years later, Greg recalls that he 'just drifted into climbing as a result of being interested in roaming around in the bush. It seemed like a better alternative to the city.' He had no interest in formal sports and other conventional hobbies, but he had, much to his parents' alarm, started collecting poisonous snakes. However, this hobby came to a premature conclusion when he was lucky to survive being bitten by a tiger snake, one of the most dangerous species in the country and one whose bite is usually fatal.

Looking for something else to occupy his time, he and a friend noticed people climbing on a cliff in the Blue Mountains outside Sydney and, Greg remembers, 'we automatically decided to figure out how to do that ourselves. We did that using a little handbook from the Boy Scouts.' He still feels that, in spite of an early traumatic accident (when a belay pulled out and catapulted him down a rock face, leaving him facing five operations to insert steel plates and screws in his smashed ankle), there is real merit in being self-taught. 'The idea of teaching yourself is important because it adds to the level of exploration,' he says, adding that he believes the best climbers to be intuitive.

In spite of a highly successful 'career', Greg admits to being ambivalent about the climbing game. It is no accident that the title of his highly acclaimed book of essays is *Mixed Emotions*, and Greg is convinced that professional climbing induces a strong element of tunnel vision to the exclusion of other activities and relationships. 'When I put all those stories together I was saying that I've got a lot to be thankful for in climbing, but it's not always good.'

The lowest point in Greg's climbing was almost certainly Pete Thexton's death during the 1983 expedition to Broad Peak (on which Andy Parkin was also a member). Thexton, a doctor in addition to being a climber, was partnering Greg and contracted pulmonary oedema near the summit. Greg was also near the limit and suffering himself from altitude sickness accompanied by blackouts. Together, the pair made a desperate descent down the mountain. After nearly 24 hours without rest, Greg thought they had reached the comparative safety of the tent at Camp Four only to witness his companion give up the struggle for life at sunrise the next morning.

In the intervening years Pete Thexton's death has stayed with Greg for a number of complex reasons, one of which may be because they had known each other only during the expedition: 'I hadn't known him long enough for him ever to burn me or anything like that,' Greg explains. 'Give a friendship long enough and you'll screw each other somehow, however much you ultimately like each other.

VIETNAM'S CLIMBING HISTORY

In December 1991 American climbers Sam Lightner, Todd Skinner and Jacob Valdez made the first rock-climbing visit to Vietnam. They climbed two routes in the Ha Long Bay region, first Return to Eternal Buddha (5.13a) then Charlie Don't Crank (5.12a). Each was a bolted sports climb on overhanging pocketed walls. They then moved to the Valley of the Dragon's Teeth in Nam Ninh province, near the town of Ninh Binh in the countryside south of Hanoi. Here they climbed Wen Tzu (5.13a) and Point (5.11b). Shortly after our visit in November–December 1996 Skinner returned to Ha Long Bay with a team of climbers and established several dozen new climbs.

In 1994 Maria Coffey and Dag Goering explored Ha Long Bay for material for Maria's book, *Three Moons in Vietnam*. They recognized immediately the potential for climbing and sea kayaking. They have run several guided kayak trips to the archipelago since then, and it was their enthusiasm, photographs and information that stimulated our trip.

It is interesting to speculate on the future of climbing in Ha Long Bay. In many respects its development will be in direct proportion to the easing of the bureaucratic nightmare that one has to endure to visit Vietnam. As tourism is promoted and increases, the situation should improve. Then, there is no reason why the region should not develop into one of world importance to climbers. It then may follow Thailand as the major climbing region of South-east Asia.

I had this almost saintly picture of him because of that'. Another reason may be because 'I'd entered this phase of climbing that is dangerous. I know people get killed here. But of course you don't really think it's going to happen to you or the guys you're with.'

Sitting on the boat off the coast of Vietnam, Greg summed up by saying: 'These things stick with you on a daily, possibly even hourly basis. It's just a thing that's burnt into you. It's not to say I'm morbid about it. It's just a thing that's part of my history and my experience. It's one of the most powerful things I know. Not only did he share his life with me; he shared his death too.'

On the other side of the equation, Greg argues that any successful trip is a relative high point but adds, 'Some have a tag on them that holds them above the others. Climbing K2 was definitely a good one.'

Along with three other climbers – Steve Swenson, Phil Ershler and Greg Mortimer – Greg reached the summit of what is often described as the world's most difficult mountain in 1990 by the north ridge. He was at a mental and physical high point:

> Getting to the top was nothing like I had thought it would be. We had clouds and fog on the summit, but then we'd suddenly look down and there would be a tunnel through the cloud. I could see Broad Peak, where Pete had died. I was looking down and thinking about him. Then you'd look over the other side and there would be some views of the west of China, which is a huge expanse of arid mountains. I remember sitting up there for a good 45 minutes on the top. There's this strange euphoria up there that makes you keep going back for more. It's intoxicating.

Yet descending, in Greg's phrase, 'slapped us into shape very quickly'. Battling through a building storm and surrounded by powder-snow avalanches, they found route-finding a nightmare. Earlier in the day one of the party, Phil Ershler, had abandoned his personal bid for the summit and was now in a tent at around 26,250 feet (8000 m). It was his light that guided the others back, and Greg believes that without it they would not have found safety, adding: 'We managed to crawl back into the tent, absolutely wrecked. It's funny how things work out. His galling defeat, so to speak, is really the reason we are alive.'

Over recent years, and with the death of many friends, Greg Child has revised his opinion about what constitutes acceptable risk:

> There was a period, around when I was going to K2, when I was incredibly gung-ho about taking risk. Before and during a trip you think you could get killed up here. And you think, 'How do I feel about that?' And you think, 'I guess I'll accept that as a necessary consequence of what trying to climb K2 involves'. Now I'm not quite so willing to take those risks as a day-to-day routine. I still go on climbs that are dangerous and have their inherent risk. But I'm more willing to back off these days. I like the idea of living, enjoying a natural demise.

Greg clearly remembers first meeting his partner Andy Parkin on the ill fated 1983 trip to Broad Peak. Greg describes him as a very self-contained person. 'Andy is fiercely independent without being overbearing about his independence, but he's very minimalist. He lives a very simple, artistic, pretty low-budget life without any trappings of the modern age.'

Andy Parkin, who was born in 1954, now describes himself as an artist rather than a climber, although he was one of the foremost Alpinists of the late 1970s and early 1980s. Born and brought up in Sheffield, he has spent the last 12 years living in the leading centre of contemporary Alpinism, Chamonix. That he is still climbing at a very high standard, undertaking bold, new routes and partnering the likes of Greg Child, is nothing short of a miracle because, in the summer of 1984, Andy suffered the most catastrophic accident.

While he was guiding, a belay collapsed when the rock broke away and the resulting accident left Andy with a smashed left elbow, a hip that was broken in 13 places and numerous other injuries, including an exploded spleen. Most frightening his heart had been forced out of its protective casing. 'Clinically, I was actually dying,' is how Andy describes it today, adding that the doctors had not previously seen anyone survive his injuries. He appears to have done so in the face of all medical opinion and of doctors who warned his family that he would not pull through. Not being in a coma helped, and he undoubtedly had been extremely fit, but Andy's attitude was a key factor in his cheating death. He talks of the power of the mind over the body and, in spite of having been treated by some excellent doctors, adds: 'Really, compared with nature, medicine has barely started. You've just got to believe in yourself, and that is what I did – just believed in myself.'

Not surprisingly, Andy was left mentally, as well as physically, scarred by the accident and it took around four years for him to recover. As he says:

It does leave you with things that you would prefer to forget. It took a long, long time to come to terms with. The lifestyle I adored was the climber's lifestyle, and suddenly I was confronted with this: the dread… less the dread of actually getting killed, more the dread of getting maimed and the fear of being paralysed for instance.

Looking back over a decade later, Andy sums up his accident with the words: 'You learn a lot of humility in a situation like that.'

At moments in Vietnam the legacy of his fall is still obvious: he walks with a pronounced limp and the left-hand side of his body, especially his arm and leg, is virtually immobile. Many people would class Andy Parkin simply as permanently disabled; predictably, he does not see his condition in that light.

Andy's climbing record is an impressive one: in the French Alps he has soloed the Droites by several lines (including its north face in an impressive five hours) and he made the first true alpine-style winter solo ascent of the Walker Spur in under 19 hours. Further afield, he joined Greg Child for a successful attempt on Broad Peak in Pakistan and has twice attempted K2 in alpine style via new routes.

Since his accident, and despite the doctors' gloomy predictions to the contrary, Andy still manages to climb at an incredibly high standard. His willingness to take risks is a hallmark of his climbing and in the winter season of 1991–2 he put up three new, bold routes in the Chamonix Aiguilles. He has also been on expeditions to Makalu and Everest, climbed Shivling and made a series of dramatic solo ascents in Patagonia. But the aftermath of Andy's accident has reawakened his interest in art and, in particular, in mountain painting, which he feels is a neglected genre. On the long road to recovery, this became particularly important as he needed to prove he could do something useful. It was, he recalls, 'a life-saver in hospital'. Today, in spite of much critical praise, Andy earns only a modest

Andy painting with ink and watercolour as the boat navigates through Ha Long Bay.
Most vessels feature a distinctive bright yellow dragon as a figure-head on their bow.

living from his paintings and sculptures. 'As far as I am concerned, I'm an artist. The accident brought home to me just how important it was and how necessary.'

In recent years Andy has developed a distinctive style: the climber Fred Harper, who knows Andy well, described his paintings of the mountains surrounding Chamonix as combining, 'an always cold blue iciness with the soaring blues and red of the granite. There is something of Andy in there too, an ore, tough, dramatic, single-minded, reaching for the sky no matter what the obstacle.'

Now, when travelling to climb, Andy thinks of both climbing and painting and what equipment he should take for both. On the trip to Vietnam, for instance, his art materials consisted of just a simple set of watercolour paints and ink to keep the weight down, but on other expeditions he will also take pastels and acrylics.

While Andy's art is now a key force in his life, climbing has always held a central place. He left school at 16 ('as fast as I could') and began an electrician's apprenticeship – although he would have preferred joinery – but after a couple of years he left to take casual jobs on building sites which paid more and meant he could get away to the Alps for long periods. Later, when the jobs were drying up in Britain, he moved to the States and worked illegally on the oil-rigs in Colorado, living, like a nomad, in a car in the desert. All the time climbing was the main focus of his life, and he only ever earned enough money to survive.

To Andy, climbing is also a means of expression and an art form in its own right. Artistically he likes to experiment with many different media and views climbing simply as an extension of this. He is convinced that his climbing comes from within and that he is following an animal-like instinct. 'You run first and ask questions afterwards.' This has manifested itself in his solo climbing and in his quest for new routes. He enjoys the former 'because you don't have any pressures' and finds it 'the ultimate form of climbing'. Often Andy discovers that he becomes obsessed with a particular route, which takes on a life of its own, becoming 'a dangerous bug that insinuates itself into your mind and you get around to accepting the idea – daring to go for it and then finding yourself on it. It is the most perfect form of climbing.'

The attraction of new routes is that of real discovery. Although Andy will travel great distances to seek out new lines, he also appreciates finding forgotten corners in the mountains above his adopted town of Chamonix which grow and become 'projects in your own imagination'.

Andy eventually managed to get a flight to Hanoi and finally both climbers were at Bai Chay preparing for the first journey out into the bay itself. Now squatting on the harbour-front, his long fair hair masking the concentration on his gaunt face, Andy was painting the bustling activity of the dockside. Around him gathered the crowd of inquisitive onlookers that artists always attract. When the motor boat finally arrived he closed his sketchbook and stood, stretching the travel stiffness from his tall, bony frame.

Chaotically, the team piled on to the boat, Greg's powerful, stocky physique obvious as he squeezed next to Andy. Their plan was to find a couple of climbs that inspired them: a warm-up route to get the feel of the place, and a hard, major undertaking that would leave a legacy for other climbers to follow.

Dag, from Canada, bearded, unkempt and looking like an ancient mariner, had been here before and acted as our guide to the labyrinth of limestone towers that stretched as far as the eye could see. Bear-like, he dwarfed the clean-shaven man from the Vietnamese Foreign Ministry who stuck with the team like a Siamese twin, allegedly to help and advise. Richard, Duncan and Keith were filming and Brian was along to take care of the climbers' safety. Then of course there was the translator and the boatman. Ten in a six-man boat!

The boat was a little low in the water as she pulled away from the harbour at the start of the search, children waving and running excitedly along the dock. After an hour, Greg and Andy still had not found their ideal routes. The boat negotiated a maze of channels, staring up at towering buttresses of white limestone. The cliffs dwarfed the sampans and junks plying beneath, their noisy motors echoing off the cliffs. Dag explained that sail had only recently been replaced by the thud of diesel engines.

The stacks and islands were usually a couple of hundred metres apart and rose up to a height of around 500 feet (150 m). Many were vegetated and the rock abstractly streaked with black where water run-off channels encouraged the growth of lichen and moss. It soon became apparent that the steeper rock was of better quality for climbing, and here beautiful chandeliers of ochre stalactites and columns of tufa adorned the overhanging limestone. There were innumerable possibilities for short one- or two-pitch climbs, but Greg and Andy were searching for something longer and more challenging.

On one occasion they turned into a low grotto. As the boat glided through they could touch its cool, crypt-like ceiling dripping with water. Bright light at its far end promised a mysterious Lost World. The boat emerged into a large collapsed cavern with shafts of sunlight illuminating the crater walls draped with vines and stalactites. Behind followed three fishermen in a coracle, inquisitive at the boat's trespass into their secret world. They laughed and shouted to the boatman as they cast their nets and retrieved a couple of well-used bamboo lobster-pots.

Later the crew passed a floating village of 50 or so small boats moored together, made of woven bamboo impregnated with tar. It was a hive of activity, children playing, mothers cooking and men repairing nets. An entire floating community. In the same bay a superb rock buttress stood guard over a narrow channel of water like a giant tombstone. Its striking colour, a glowing orange, was reflected in the water, and deep black fissures defined a logical line up the imposing slab.

The rock embodied everything Greg and Andy were looking for in a warm-up climb. The climbers could follow crack lines, where they would find plenty of natural protection, valuable time would not have to be spent preparing the route, and it could be climbed in a relatively fluid style in two lengths of rope. Andy summed it up: 'Elegant and very aesthetic. A classic line. You look at it and want to climb it.'

In the afternoon the team was heading back from an area of stacks in one of the main channels of the west sector of Ha Long Bay when the boat turned into an inlet containing a magnificent wall on a tower that leant drunkenly at an absurd angle. Fortuitously, the limestone had been formed then weathered at the perfect angle for a desperate modern rock-climb. The boat edged closer to the face. Andy and Greg craned their heads backwards, excitedly pointing out different lines on the overhanging pocketed wall slashed with roofs and grooves embellished with stalactites and pillars of limestone tufa deposits. They realized quickly that the most elegant and outstanding feature on which to concentrate their efforts was a big prow towards the left side of the face.

Satisfied that the climbs had been found, the team headed back. The following morning the team boarded a larger boat which provided living accommodation while they attempted the climbs. Andy's and Greg's first objective was to return to climb the route they had christened Tombstone Wall, which turned out to be the perfect starter: two naturally protected pitches that tested them just enough.

The morning after Tombstone Wall had been climbed the boat sailed to the leaning tower which they named Valhalla Island. Once there, she edged close to the back of the tower, the ornate yellow dragon figurehead grating on the rough limestone as she fought against the unpredictable currents around the stack. When the boat was in position, the safety rigging team who were fixing the ropes for the filming, climbed the back of the stack, which sloped at an amenable angle, enabling the summit to be gained without too much difficulty. From the top they dropped a rope down the intended line of the route; it fell 165 feet (50 m) to the sea and its bottom end was 50 feet (15 m) away from the rock. From the boat, now anchored below the steep side, Greg and Andy managed to reach the rope then climbed it using ascenders, inspecting every inch of their proposed route. They tried to visualize the climb, the moves from hold to hold, and the protection they would need. Would they be able to use natural threads, nuts and cams or would they have to place bolts? What were the best positions for the belays and how many pitches would they have to divide the climb into? Who would lead which pitch? There were holds but virtually nowhere to rest. Would they have the physical fitness to climb the route in good style without rest or aid? The task was daunting, but it looked just possible.

Back on the boat and conscious of the ethical debate, they discussed the use of bolts. Greg summed up their conclusions in typical understatement:

> I have no problems at all with bolts. I put up a lot of new routes in Australia and the States in the 1980s and I still do a few now which are often bolted sports routes. These steep limestone cliffs lend themselves to bolting, and after all you cannot be worried environmentally about a few bits of metal sticking out of these cliffs when you consider all the lead that was dropped on this country in the war.

There was a danger that Andy and Greg would exhaust themselves before the climb if they did all the preparation, and as time was short the safety rigging team

Greg seconding the first pitch of Boat People. It was near the top of the picture where Andy pulled the flake off and fell, howling towards the sea. Their base camp boat is anchored behind.

helped by preparing the upper three pitches. Normally, on rock of such difficulty the route is prepared from the top before the actual climb, as it is much quicker and safer to abseil down the route, removing loose rock and dirt, finding protection points and organizing belays from the security of the rope. Because the wall was so overhanging this job proved to be very strenuous. Frequently, they had to swing into the rock and tie back the rope or they would find themselves spinning uselessly in space. The access to the diagonal first pitch was very difficult, so Andy and Greg worked on this by climbing from the sea.

Before Andy and Greg could start the first pitch they had to reach a small shelf above the water. When safe, they sorted out all their equipment, but the weight of the extra gear needed for climbing a new route was a severe handicap for such a strenuous pitch: two sets of nuts, a full range of camming devices, pegs, hammer, numerous nylon slings, quick-draws and several dozen karabiners, all critical to their safety and success as they were going into unknown territory.

Andy had drawn the short straw for the first pitch. He started by climbing from pocket to pocket then up a finger crack. The angle looked improbable and climbing it was possible only because there were plenty of big holds. From the start his strength was drained by the overhanging rock. He contorted his body to come closer to the rock and bring the weight on to his legs. Trying to rest, he hung on with one hand for what seemed like an eternity, struggling to place a couple of decent nuts for protection.

Nagging at the back of his mind was the nightmare of climbing into a blind alley and being unable to retreat, and deep down he even wondered if the climb was possible. All it needed was a short distance without any holds and progress would be stopped abruptly.

Greg patiently held the rope on the belay shelf, alternating his attention from Andy to the growing group of inquisitive local boat people, who stared wide-eyed and unbelieving at the crazy Westerners' antics. Andy by now had reached an area of blocky rock 40 feet (12 m) above and to the right of the shelf. He cleaned off one or two loose rocks and was left with a fragile flake. With strength running out he was in a dilemma: would the flake hold? Could he dare use it? One way or the other he had to make a decision quickly. He gingerly lowered his weight on to the hold and then put a sling over the flake. Just as he was about to clip the rope into

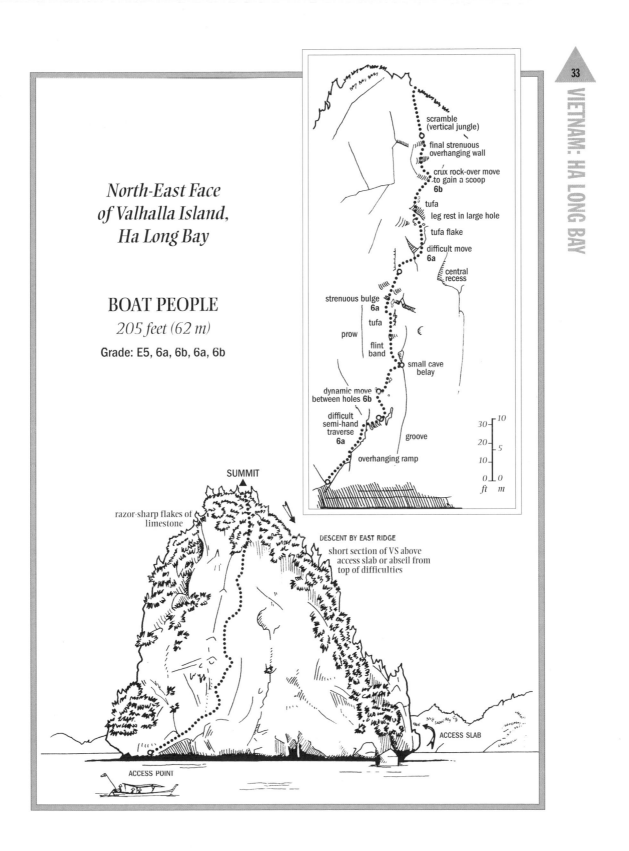

North-East Face
of Valhalla Island,
Ha Long Bay

BOAT PEOPLE

205 feet (62 m)

Grade: E5, 6a, 6b, 6a, 6b

scramble
(vertical jungle)

final strenuous
overhanging wall

crux rock-over move
to gain a scoop
6b

tufa

leg rest in large hole

tufa flake

difficult move
6a

central
recess

strenuous bulge
6a

tufa

prow

flint
band

small cave
belay

dynamic move
between holes **6b**

difficult
semi-hand
traverse
6a

groove

overhanging ramp

SUMMIT

razor-sharp flakes of
limestone

DESCENT BY EAST RIDGE

short section of VS above
access slab or absell from
top of difficulties

ACCESS SLAB

ACCESS POINT

Andy regained the rock after falling and led the first pitch successfully. Notice the nuts, cams and krabs hanging from his harness which are used to protect the climb.

the sling there was a sickening creak, then a sudden crack and the whole flake came away. Andy recalls:

I exploded backwards, falling with the big flake cradled in my arms, howling towards the sea. Instinctively, I let go of it just in time before it pulled me with it. When we parted it crashed into the water like a bomb, and I went hurtling under the roof. It flashed through my mind as I fell: why am I still falling; has the protection pulled or has the belay failed?

The rope stretched then held as Andy's feet brushed the water. Both climbers were surprised by the length of the fall. Thirty feet (9 m), but it seemed more.

Andy was lucky. The rock had narrowly missed cutting his rope, and it was only because the wall was so undercut and overhanging that he was not flung against the rock as his body plummeted towards the sea.

They now had an audience of half a dozen boats full of bemused fishing folk. Obviously, the word was out that some strange ritual was going on. The little children were particularly taken with Andy hanging limp, like an out-of-work puppet, above the sea.

Afterwards Andy remembered feeling relief, in a strange way glad that he had fallen. The natural instinct is to fear falling, but on overhanging rock the fall was safely into space and by surviving he had got the fear out of his system and could relax to perform better on the route.

Andy tied a couple of prusik knots around the rope and ascended it with their aid. He then climbed back up to the high point and managed to get more good nut and thread protection. Above was a strange tufa formation. These were common on the rock faces in the area and often formed weird organ-pipe structures and beautiful free-hanging stalactites produced by the solution then redeposition of limestone. At first they felt strange, but with care they provided excellent holds on otherwise blank and overhanging rock. Andy gave the tufa a couple of knocks to test it. The hollow reply was not very reassuring. 'They're always stronger than they look,' Andy convinced himself, and climbed the tufa into an alcove where he placed a peg and in a contorted way managed to half-rest.

He continued his ascent but soon reached an impasse and had to come down. This wasted a tremendous amount of strength, and he started to wonder whether he had the stamina to complete the pitch. Another peg for protection and his confidence started to return. The only option was out to the right, around a nose of rock by a wild, hanging semi-hand traverse. This required an extremely physical style of climbing where most of the body was supported by the arms, the stomach muscles straining to attempt to hold the legs onto the rock, allowing some weight to be transferred through the feet. Arms at near exhaustion point, Andy drove his body on. It was touch and go, and the last moves on to the belay were the hardest.

On the belay a broad grin grew on Andy's face, then he threw back his head and laughed. 'Brilliant!'

Bemused boat people watch the crazy Westerners as they climb. Their small craft serves as transport, accommodation and fishing boat.

Afterwards, still smiling, he summed up the pitch enthusiastically as 'very fine climbing, great, and very exciting. It felt hard leading, cleaning, putting protection and pegs in on the lead. English 6a, perhaps harder, but you never know the first time.'

Back on the boat that evening, over a sumptuous seafood banquet of fish, crabs and prawns, the next day's attempt on the climb was discussed down to the smallest detail. An early start was vital if they were going to complete the climb on the following day.

The next morning was cloudy – perfect, as the weather would not be too hot, even though the climb faced north-east, protecting it from the semitropical sun.

Knowledge of a climb certainly makes things easier, and Andy and Greg quickly climbed the first pitch. Andy still felt it to be technically hard and strenuous, but now he had no doubt about whether the pitch was possible or which exact line the route would take. Above was a different matter. They had imagined the climb a hundred times the night before, but they could make only experienced guesses as to whether their plan would work in reality. At least the loose rock had been cleared and vital protection points were in place – that is, assuming the route went where they planned.

The pitch above was highlighted by two peculiar deep holes a foot across and over an arm's span apart. There were holds above and below – but how to reach between the holes? Greg climbed strenuously to the first hole, on the way clipping two bolts for protection. By turning upside-down he then managed to get the whole of his left leg into the hole, hoping that no bats or tropical beasts lurked in its depths. In this bizarre position he managed to take his hands off and effect a welcome rest on the 25-degree overhanging wall. Word had got around that the crazy Westerners were again performing and a dozen boats and coracles were now under the climb. When Greg performed his antics a huge roar of laughter erupted from the audience. One bearded old fisherman even turned upside-down in the bottom of his tiny coracle and waved his leg in the air trying to mimic Greg's position.

The crowd fell silent as Greg planned his next crucial moves. A hold the size of a small matchbox was the only feature between the holes – far too small to hang his weight on but perhaps big enough to help. Greg took his leg from the hole, reached for the 'matchbox' and got two fingertips on it. With his left leg and arm bunched on the edge of the hole and his right leg smearing the smooth rock for friction, he was like a coiled spring ready for release. Cat-like he leapt, his timing and aim perfect. His fingers just managed to reach the higher hole and curl around the edge as the rest of his body lost contact with the rock. He swung wildly as tendons and muscles strained to hold the hard-won edge with one hand. Quickly, he pulled up to the better holds above and then to the security of the second belay in a small cave.

Andy now followed, normally an easier proposition than leading, with the security of the rope above preventing a fall of any distance. Unfortunately, due to Andy's past injuries the next moves proved virtually impossible. He could neither rest in the hole nor bunch his body for the dynamic leap. Instead he tried to hold all his weight on the 'matchbox' hold. It did not work and he fell, swinging clear of the rock as the rope held him. The audience in the boats thought this great fun and, innocent of the serious predicament above, cheered as Andy tried to make contact with the rock.

With great difficulty he managed to regain the rock then try the moves again only to fall once more. The laughter and expectant chatter from below reached new levels and you almost expected them to shout 'Encore'. Andy was despondent and exhausted. With strength for one last attempt he tried a new tactic. By using a bizarre combination of virtually nonexistent holds he positioned his body and, with every tendon stretched to breaking point, just managed to reach the elusive second pocket.

Andy rested his shattered arms and fingers in the confines of the cave belay. It was now his turn to take the lead. He leant backwards, craning his neck to look at the way above. The best line was not obvious.

He felt a great sense of exposure as he left the airy perch of the cave. The rock was potentially friable, consisting of a band of hard, shiny flint sticking out of the limestone. Andy was hesitant, dubious about trusting the flint and unsure of his physical reserves after the débâcle below. Once committed, the climbing turned out to be easier than expected, and with growing confidence he reached a small roof with a good thread runner for protection. The wall was still leaning out, so unfortunately he could not rest. Speed was vital before his strength ran out but to rush could easily lead to a mistake.

His error was a common one in climbing. Above was a slot in which he placed a small camming device. In his haste it twisted as he put it in and did not give the planned protection for the difficult moves above. Strenuously hanging on with one hand, he could not correct the placement. With strength again running out Andy had to move but found that the cam had completely blocked the crucial hold. He made a valiant attempt to use a small hold above but could not make the vital pull. The fall took a long time coming. At first it looked as though he would make it back down to the safety of the good thread, but his arms turned to jelly. In panic he tried to remove the cam so he could use the hold it blocked, but his fingers could not hold on any longer and he plummeted into space. The rope did its work as it first stretched to absorb his weight then held the fall. Andy was getting used to hanging in space.

Back on the rock, Andy made a determined attempt to remove the offending cam. Eventually, it came out after a struggle, and this time, with the help of the vital finger slot, the moves were relatively straightforward. Above, the angle eased to vertical. The respite in difficulty was a godsend, as by this time Andy's reserves of energy were past the empty mark.

In retrospect Andy said philosophically:

I was annoyed at my mistake, but you don't know what the hell is happening when you are going into the unknown. I chose the wrong combinations of holds, and because of the steepness it was a case of do it first time or blow it and fall off.

I normally specialize in adventurous mountain routes, and it was great to feel the same nervous sensation of launching out on this route. The difference is that you can't push it to the limit in the mountains because you have to avoid falling at all costs. Occasionally, you take a fall on these mixed or ice routes and they always seem horrendous: the inaccessibility, poor protection and the possibility of serious injury exacerbated by all the sharp ice gear hanging off you. When you are rock-climbing you are stripped

The climbers high above the sea on Boat People. Greg is belayed in a cave while Andy starts to lead the third pitch. A group of local fishermen look on.

down to a minimum and can perform near your limit. A consequence of operating at your limit is falling off. It felt good, but I had to change my attitude.

Greg joined Andy on the third belay and they prepared for the final pitch. It looked awesome! The whole pitch was just short of 100 feet (30 m); it overhung continuously, and the top third hanging above them was more a roof than a wall. Even if the holds were huge the pitch would be the crux of the climb.

Speed was essential on this gymnastic pitch. High above the sea, Greg powered up the pitch, clipping the bolts placed earlier; arms pulling and legs swinging he reached a tufa flake, which was followed by a partial leg rest in another large hole, and then it was the top roof. The crux turned out to be a dynamic rock-over move where he swung his right leg out and up to shoulder level, then acrobatically levered upwards to transfer his weight on to his legs, at the same time reaching for a small hold. On his first try, the elusive hold was out of reach and he had to

TRAVELLING TO VIETNAM

Perhaps the easiest way for European travellers to fly to Hanoi is via Hong Kong. In 1996 Air Vietnam introduced a new fleet of aeroplanes with Western-trained pilots offering a high standard of service on this final leg of the journey.

Vietnam is a country undergoing rapid change, but tourism is still a relatively new industry and a number of bureaucratic obstacles can trip up the unwary and impatient traveller – especially when language problems can complicate matters. Similarly, the word of one official in Hanoi will not necessarily be accepted by another in Ha Long Bay. Of course, independent travel is always possible, but such arrangements may well fall foul of the official systems, with resulting delays. Similarly, climbers should be aware that local officials can be mystified about their sport and worried about what they see as its inherent foolhardiness and danger.

One solution is to use the services of a local operator to make all arrangements and obtain permissions (the use of the plural is not accidental). While this may appear more expensive, a good operator can save a lot of heartache when time is limited. Mr Tue (pronounced 'Tw-ay') of Hanoi Tours is very well connected with local officials and has excellent English. As a bonus he can be e-mailed at: hanoi!tuetour@netnam.org.vn@postbox.anu.edu.au scurry back to the leg rest – vital energy wasted. On the second try he reached the hold. The top of the tower was only 15 feet (4¹⁄2 m) above, but to the drained Greg it looked much further.

The holds were bigger now and Greg drove his body on. 'I actually started to fumble. I had emptied myself of arm strength completely. I tried to clip the last bolt twice but my arms were so tired that they were wobbling and I just deflected off the bolt hanger. My aim was bad. I made a last-gasp attempt to pull round the final bit, but I had reached the point where I had nothing left to give.'

He fell from the last move, swinging harmlessly into space, his pride hurt but his body intact. After a short rest hanging on the rope, he pulled himself up to the bolt that had held the fall, and completed the climb. With arms rested, the last moves were not that hard.

The sun had set and the lights from hundreds of small fishing boats reflected from the calm, ink-coloured sea by the time Andy joined Greg on the top. It had been a long time since they had climbed together in the different world of the Himalayas. But then, as now, they shared the intense emotional satisfaction and physical exhaustion that only climbing brings.

They named the route Boat People.

Andy (left) and Greg relax on the boat after the successful ascent of Boat People.

Tony Howard and Di Taylor

Wadi Rum, Jordan

2

A third of the way up the climb their progress was halted by an imposing wide crack that they later christened aptly 'the bloody awful chimney'. Tony knew it was going to be a fight and remembers it vividly to this day:

It was smooth on the inside and smooth on the outside, narrowing as I went up. It was like a three-moves-up and two-moves-down job. Pushing me out, no gear in, pulling me down, getting narrower. Climb up and slither down. Red hot and sweat dripping off me, gasping for breath, no runners, and no idea where I was going, because all that was above me was this bloody great big overhang.

Eventually, about 10 feet (3 m) below the overhang I found an unexpected little ledge on the right wall which I pulled out onto, feeling very small, I had no gear in at all – no runners in front, no runners behind.

Di Taylor leads the diagonal crack which was the only weakness in the upper slab of the Haj.

What the hell was I going to do now? I looked up and saw that the roof crack might fit my largest cam. So I plucked up courage and reluctantly squeezed back into the chimney. It was a fight all the way up to the roof. Relief came at last as the piece of protection sank into the crack and I dropped back down on to the ledge for a breather, sweating like hell, knackered really.

Tony was then perched, eagle-like, 500 feet (152 m) above the hot, shimmering desert floor of Jordan. The nearest settlement was many hours' drive north, but only native Bedouin travel in this area and even they do so infrequently. This is one of the most isolated places in the whole Wadi Rum desert but somewhere that Lancashire climbers Tony Howard and Di Taylor have, in Di's own words, 'made a second home'. Today, very few places are truly remote, and you can leave Britain in the early morning and be in Wadi Rum village by late afternoon. A flight of four hours is followed by a road journey lasting a similar time, yet remoteness is measured not only in distance and time. Immediately you leave the capital, Amman, and head due south for Wadi Rum, it is obvious that Jordan is still relatively poor. Consisting of just over four million inhabitants (of whom more than a million are estimated to be Palestinian refugees), the country is largely arid with comparatively little natural wealth, and one that struggles to balance its financial affairs.

WEATHER AND SEASONS

The temperature is the main consideration when planning the timing of a trip to Wadi Rum. Mid-May to mid-September is far too hot for climbing, with temperatures in excess of 40˚C. December to March are much cooler, with the chance of the occasional shower and flash flood. Unfortunately, the days at this time of year are very short. The ideal time is October and April, when there are lovely daytime temperatures of around 30˚C, cooler nights and little chance of precipitation. Many people prefer the spring, as the days are longer – from 5 a.m. to 7.30 p.m. – and water is more abundant than in the autumn and the desert floor is green and carpeted with flowers.

Allow a few days to acclimatize to the dry, hot atmosphere and always carry plenty of water, as dehydration can be a serious problem.

You leave the confines of the city almost immediately but it is at least two-thirds of the journey before the flat, mainly monotone landscape takes on a more mountainous aspect. Although the road gets smaller once you have turned off the main Amman to Aqaba highway at Quweirah, it is only when you near Wadi Rum village itself that any sense of the country's true splendour is revealed. While the ruined capital of the Nabataeans at Petra remains Jordan's principal attraction (and indeed one of the most important sites in the whole of the Middle East), Wadi Rum comes a close second. It is named after the largest of an intricate net-work of *wadis* (valleys), which for centuries have been used as trade routes through this jumbled landscape. In the last decade Wadi Rum has become a prime tourist destination, and it is not hard to see why, for almost everyone who has visited here has been drawn to both the landscape and to the native Bedouin.

These proud, independent people are members of the Howeitat tribe, and they view themselves as the most traditional of all the Jordanian tribes. Only in recent years have they begun to change from a semi-nomadic existence, living in black tents in the desert, to that of settling in a permanent community. They fit in perfectly with a land-scape where shattered sandstone pillars and isolated massifs rise dramatically upwards from the desert floor and, massed one after the other, vanish away into the distance. The desert 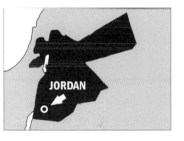 floor is itself some 3000 feet (915 m) above sea-level with Jebel Rum at 5755 feet (1754 m) the highest mountain in the central massif, soaring majestically above the village. This is an area that has seen rapid development since Tony Howard and Di Taylor first came here in 1984. At that time the Rest House, now used by climbers and tourists alike, had no electricity, no water and, unlike today, no telephone or fax. The village consisted of little more than a cluster of Bedouin in tents around six houses given by the king to the desert sheikhs, together with an almost surreal, tiny battlemented fort from which the desert police mounted their patrols. Now, visitors are greeted by an unsightly and rapidly expanding village that, unless controlled, could ultimately be spoilt by haphazard development.

Surprisingly, in the past the area was virtually ignored by climbers, although there was one notable ascent in 1952. Other climbers had visited the region on holiday but seemingly failed to realize its potential. However, Tony seeing David

Lean's *Lawrence of Arabia* at the cinema, was captivated immediately by the Middle East and began reading *Seven Pillars of Wisdom* for any information it might inadvertently contain about climbing. Lawrence himself visited Wadi Rum time and again during the Arab revolt of 1917–18, and beneath his florid prose lies a remarkably accurate assessment of the area:

> We looked up to the left to a long wall of rock, sheering in like a thousand-foot wave towards the middle of the valley; whose other arc, to the right, was an opposing line of steep, red broken hills. We rode up the slope, crashing our way through the brittle undergrowth.
>
> …The hills on the right grew taller and sharper, a fair counterpart of the other side, which straightened itself to one massive rampart of redness. They drew together until only 2 miles divided them: and then, towering gradually till their parallel parapets must have been a thousand feet above us, ran forward in an avenue for miles.
>
> They were not unbroken walls of rock, but were built sectionally, in crags like gigantic buildings, along the two sides of their street. Deep alleys, 50 feet across, divided the crags, whose plans were smoothed by the weather into huge apses and bays, and enriched with surface fretting and fracture, like design. Caverns high up on the precipice were round like windows: others near the foot gaped like doors. Dark stains ran down the shadowed front for hundreds of feet, like accidents of use. The cliffs were striated vertically, in their granular rock; whose main order stood on 200 feet of broken stone deeper in colour and harder in texture. This plinth did not, like the sandstone, hang in folds like cloth; but chipped itself into loose courses of scree, horizontal as the footing of a wall.

Although there is no record that Lawrence explored these mountains, he neverthe-less appears to have been acutely aware of their presence. Tony and Di have also been fascinated by desert landscapes, exploring those in Iran, Oman and right

▶ **Sabbah Atieeq crossing the crucial traverse on Sabbah's Route while Tony Howard and Di Taylor watch and belay. He is protected from falling into the *siq* below by bolts placed several years ago.**

JORDAN'S CLIMBING HISTORY

Before 1984 there was no serious climbing on Wadi Rum. Sheikh Hamdan took cartographers to the summit of Jebel Rum in 1949 and guided British climbers Longstaff and Banford when they made the first European ascent of Jebel Rum in 1952. His son Hammad followed in his father's footsteps and repeated many of the traditional Bedouin routes.

Tony Howard became inquisitive about the climbing possibilities of the area after seeing the film *Lawrence of Arabia*, some of which was shot in the region. He spent a considerable amount of time and energy trying to persuade the Jordanian government to allow climbing here and was finally rewarded in 1984 when they invited him to visit. In October of that year, Tony, together with Di Taylor, Mick Shaw and Alan Baker, started exploring the area and, with the help of the friendly Bedouin, discovered a number of Bedouin classics such as Hammad's Route and also several new routes, including the first ascent of the previously unclimbed Jebel Kharazeh.

During the following couple of years the British team was joined by French guide Wilfried Colonna, and together they began climbing the modern classics of Wadi Rum with ascents of Inshallah Factor and Pillar of Wisdom and the discovery of Sabbah's Route. Then the Swiss climbers Claude and Yves Remy arrived and started a period of intense exploration, starting with exciting new routes on the previously unclimbed twin peaks of Nassrani.

In 1986, at Tony and Di's instigation, the Ministry of Tourism hosted an International Guides Meet and the valley received its first invasion of teams from the UK and Europe. Many new areas were opened, such as Barrah Canyon, and the standard of the climbs continued to rise with the ascents such as Towering Inferno (graded ED inf) and Ziggurat (graded 7a). Rowland and Mark Edwards were particularly inspired by the area and returned the following year to climb a trio of hard climbs: Sandstorm, Lionheart and Warriors of the Wastelands.

More recently, the Austrians Haupolter and Precht have been the driving force in raising new standards. In particular the pair made four ascents of the highest standard in 1990 with Never Say Never, Jolly Joker, Corner Line and Incredible Possibility. In 1992 controversy hit the valley when a Spanish team used 39 bolts on Revienta o Burila.

In the relatively short period of 15 years Wadi Rum has become an important and popular venue for climbers from all nationalities. Most visitors repeat routes, choosing from the legacy of hundreds of quality climbs of all difficulties. Although the main wave of exploration is finished, the original Anglo–French team continues to search for new climbs, the Haj being a fine example of their recent exploratory efforts.

Full details of routes are found in the third edition (1997) of Tony Howard's guide, *Treks and Climbs in Wadi Rum, Jordan* (Cicerone Press).

across North Africa from Ethiopia and the Sudan all the way to Morocco. When they contacted the Jordanian government, they were eventually invited out by the Ministry of Tourism to assess Wadi Rum's potential for climbers and trekkers.

Tony and Di have known each other since childhood, and they have been partners on and off the rock for over 20 years. Both were brought up in the small industrial village of Greenfield, some 5 miles (8 km) to the east of Oldham and in the shadow of the Pennine moors, but it is their love of climbing that binds Tony and Di together. For up to six months in any year they will be abroad and, during their time in Britain, most weekends are spent climbing in the Pennines, the Peak District and North Wales. Most revealingly, they prefer to climb almost exclusively with each other, and years of partnership on the rock mean that they have developed their own intuitive style. They climb calmly and quietly together, taking great delight from each other's presence.

Di talks of the climbing-rope being 'a cord between us' from which she can feel every move, while Tony observes: 'Once I have led off, there may be very little conversation until we top out because we know exactly what each other's doing. It boils down to perfect trust, in fact.'

Climbing is central to both their lives, and Tony freely admits to having always preferred climbing to working. 'Climbing has been the whole of my life. It has been the basis for everything I've done. I consider myself a climber above everything else.'

This is reflected in Tony's 'career'. He disregarded parental advice about taking up a university place and later left his job in a pathology laboratory when the introduction of weekend working threatened his free time. 'Much to my parents' dismay I jacked in the idea of university and went off to South Georgia and around the Antarctic for six months on a whaling ship – which now sounds awful, but back in 1958 everybody assumed that whales would last for ever. There wasn't the same environmental awareness that there is now. I signed on as a mess boy, and I ended up being the doctor's assistant and poking around in people's appendices and ruptured spleens.'

▶ Sabbah leads Di and Tony along the broad ridge that eventually led to the summit of Jebel Rum. The sun is setting behind storm clouds and higher up they found a convenient bivouac site to spend the night.

Later, he continued climbing while on the dole or working at outdoor centres in the summer months. His wanderlust also saw him working in the Yukon for a couple of years and undertaking a 1000-mile (1610-km) canoe trip right through the unpeopled Northwest Territories of Canada. As a climber he has been active in Britain (particularly on Pennine grit and limestone), but he is best known for his climbing abroad, which has almost always been of an exploratory nature and even today he is still remembered for the first ascent of Norway's Troll Wall in 1965.

Like his subsequent climbing in Jordan, Tony has a knack of looking for new routes away from the crowds. 'Not many people really knew about Norway because everybody was going out to Chamonix. A couple of us went out in the winter of 1964 and, as there was quite a bit of snow on it, we were able to pick out the line of a route. So a small team from the Rimmon Climbing Club in Saddleworth went out that summer to do the climb simply because it looked like a good one.'

However, enormous publicity was generated when the media discovered that a Norwegian team also hoped to make the first ascent and promoted it as a race between the two countries. 'We became quite notorious for a long time. I wasn't happy about this because I am a person who likes to go off into quiet places and do my own thing. But it was an excellent climb. It is one of the biggest walls in Europe and a real achievement.'

Tony admits that the publicity did have one useful side-effect in enabling him and two friends to launch an equipment manufacturing company (not surprisingly named Troll), where he was a director for many years.

In reality, Tony was a reluctant entrepreneur, and as Troll grew to employ over 50 people, he realized that his directorship had become more than just a means of paying the mortgage. What had begun as a way of funding a climbing lifestyle had made increasingly more demands and eaten into his leisure time. In 1995 Tony accepted, 'with great relief', an offer to sell the company; although he and Di Taylor still retain an interest in it, they now have more free time.

Tony's wiry frame and goatee beard do much to camouflage his 57 years; Di also looks younger than her years, helped by her flowing hair, relaxed manner and carefree personality. She was attracted to climbing initially by the thriving social scene that accompanies it. Later, she devoted herself to bringing up her three children from a previous relationship (she is now, somewhat improbably, a grandmother to another three), and while they were growing up she ran a smallholding. Di returned to climbing when her children were teenagers and now climbs as hard as she has ever done. Her motivation is clear: 'It is the actual challenge. I'm not a hard climber, but getting to the top and looking at the view is my challenge.'

Their favourite area is undoubtedly Wadi Rum, about which Tony is a persuasive advocate: 'You are in a remote place where there is no rescue. In this part of the world, finding a way back off the mountain can also be extremely difficult, so it is the sense of adventure, of solitude, of exploration and, of course, the people.'

That sense of isolation was even more pronounced when Tony Howard and Di Taylor, together with two friends, Alan Baker and Mick Shaw, came here for their first climb in the mid-1980s. By then most of the peaks in the region had been climbed only by the Bedouin while they were hunting ibex or collecting edible or medicinal plants and herbs. The Bedouin enjoy climbing and are rightly proud of these unique routes as some involve complex route-finding and are relatively serious, considering they climbed barefoot and without any specialist equipment. Historically, their climbs easily compare with those of the Alpine chamois-hunters and crystal-gatherers, or the seabird-hunters of the West Coast of Scotland.

On Tony and Di's first visit to the area they had been amazed by these routes and their rediscovery gave them particular pleasure. They still climb regularly with the Bedouin, and in particular with Sabbah Atieeq. He is Jordan's most experienced climber, whose flowing, sun-bleached robes hide a strong wiry Bedouin of indeterminate middle age who clambers over the *siqs* (narrow, steep-sided gorges) and cliffs as gracefully and skilfully as the ibex he used to hunt. He knows the area intimately and is often employed by visiting climbers as a guide. Like all his kin, he is always there to help with a smile and an encouraging word.

On this visit Tony and Di planned two routes of contrasting styles which reflected their enthusiasm for both traditional Bedouin routes and modern, technically hard rock-climbs. First they would team up with their old friend Sabbah for a two-day traverse of Jebel Rum. This is one of the area's greatest Bedouin expedition routes going from west to east, climbing Sabbah's Route and then descending Hammad's Route. Then, for their second climb, they would travel far south to the Haj to climb one of the most remote desert rock-climbs by a difficult route they had pioneered a couple of years earlier.

t was still dark when Tony, Di and Sabbah woke to the haunting sound of the Muezzin's call to prayer, emanating from the small mosque in the centre of the village and echoing off the surrounding rock walls.

'Sabbah al Khayr' ('Good morning'), Sabbah greeted Tony and Di as he joined them for breakfast of coffee, chapatis, yoghurt and jam at the Rest House. With rucksacks packed with rope, a small selection of climbing gear, sleeping-bag, food and a lot of water, they were soon on their way in a four-wheel-drive Land Cruiser, the new, preferred form of desert transport which has replaced the camel as the Bedouin ship of the desert. A bumpy, dusty hour-long journey took them to the other side of the mountain, where from the flat desert floor rose abruptly, through black scree, huge battlements of red and yellow sandstone separated by deep gashes of *siqs* hewn from the rock by infrequent storm water.

Sabbah pointed out the route, which followed the largest of the *siqs* into the heart of the mountain. Then, when it came to a precipitous dead end, they would exit up the right-hand side walls on to the skyline ridge that led to the distant summit.

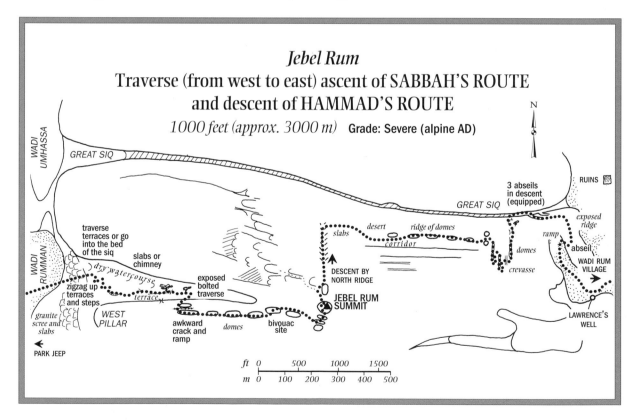

Jebel Rum
Traverse (from west to east) ascent of SABBAH'S ROUTE and descent of HAMMAD'S ROUTE
1000 feet (approx. 3000 m) **Grade: Severe (alpine AD)**

The early start had paid dividends as the sun was still hidden behind the bulk of the mountain, and they made quick progress up the uneven granite scree that forms the base of many of these peaks. At the junction with the sandstone the ground steepened and they stopped to rest, their height gain rewarding them with a magnificent view across the open valley below. Sabbah, a man of few words but with a glowing smile, looked into the distance at a small cloud of dust. 'Bedouin camp. Not many people living in tents now. Living in the village in house with jeep,' he said.

After a drink they started to climb again. To their left was the *siq* that indicated the general direction of the route, but Sabbah, who was now in front, avoided the temptation of traversing into the bed of the ravine, knowing that higher barriers caused by dried waterfalls made it unclimbable. Instead, he traversed the side walls, where 30-foot (9-m) bands of steeper rock alternated with terraces. By climbing cracks, chimneys or slabs which formed weaknesses in these cliffs, then moving along terraces, he zigzagged his way up the right side (true left bank) of the *siq*, getting ever deeper into the dark, cool shadows of the canyon. The route-finding was complex, but Sabbah had been this way many times before and was also aided by small cairns placed by the Bedouin to mark crucial points of their routes. On some of the difficult rock steps the Bedouin had piled stones below to make 'steps' to give the climbers an easier ascent; occasionally, makeshift ladders made from stout branches were jammed in otherwise holdless cracks – those with no handholds or footholds.

Di (left), Tony (centre) and Sabbah sit round a brush-wood fire at their bivouac site on Jebel Rum.

IBEX AND OTHER ANIMALS

Today, the Bedouin tend to ignore the ban on hunting ibex, although they are slowly recognizing the value of conservation. But hunting this beautiful and rarely seen animal was probably the main reason why the Bedouin became expert climbers, by venturing into the high *jebels* (mountains) which are its habitat. Like a big-game hunter and in a macho way the Bedouin are fascinated by this secretive animal, and the slightest movement in far-off rocks creates excitement and the reaching for their guns. Unfortunately, an estimated 20 ibex are shot annually around Wadi Rum alone. How long they will continue to survive this hunting remains to be seen, but protecting them is one of Tony's strongest arguments for turning the area into a national park.

Other animals that would benefit from protection are snakes, lizards, jackal, hyrax, gerbils, jirds and sand cats, together with a large variety of birds, including several species of vultures, buzzards and eagles, the most important of which are the only nesting pair of rare Verreaux's eagles in the Middle East.

Some desert animals are dangerous and in particular a bite from a viper could be fatal, although fortunately they are rarely seen. Scorpions can give a nasty sting and are occasionally found, especially under stones.

Higher, the bed of the *siq* was the easier alternative, and they made rapid progress up its sandy base. Occasionally, they had to beat a path through spiny bushes that clung to life, until the next cloudburst would replenish their water supply. Sometimes the three climbers had to negotiate their way past perfectly circular basins polished smooth by water, and as they gained height they put the rope on to protect themselves as they climbed a particularly smooth and troublesome cleft.

They stopped for lunch at a ledge deep in the canyon, marked by a gnarly juniper tree, below a hanging crack with a Bedouin 'step' at its base. In front the *siq* ended in black, precipitous walls, so they now had to climb the steep side walls. This was the most difficult part of the route, as it traversed a virtually holdless slab for 150 feet (46 m) towards the right-hand skyline highlighted in the midday sun. Tony led the way across the slab sandwiched between cliffs above and below. Any slip could have been catastrophic had it not been for the bolts that protected him from falling into the depths of the huge, dark, crevasse-like *siq* below.

Originally, when Sabbah first climbed this route he did not use a rope or any safeguards to protect himself from a slip, such was his confidence in his ability. Perhaps his climbing was so natural and second nature to him that he never thought to doubt himself. When asked why he climbed, he looked puzzled, as though he did not understand the question, then answered in his broken English 'I like the ibex.' But was he referring to his love of hunting or comparing himself to an ibex?

Controversially, several years ago Tony, Di and their friend Wilfried Colonna, a guide from France, had drilled half a dozen bolts into the slab to protect the climbers by minimizing the length of a potential fall. This decision was not taken lightly, and they canvassed opinion among the Bedouin and European climbers before placing the bolts and had to consider that the route was becoming one of the most popular objectives for visiting parties, some far less competent than others.

Tony summed up their bolting dilemma:

A slip in the middle of the slab would almost certainly result in serious injury with little hope of rescue. Against the possible loss of life we had to balance the minimal environmental damage, which only climbers would see, and the ethical dilemma of changing the character of the route. Safety won, and I'm glad, but that does not mean that I am in favour of bolts – far from it. I am very much against the widespread use of bolts, but each case has to be analysed separately. Hopefully, this will keep other Bedouin climbs free of guided parties and leave them in the solitude they deserve.

Di and Sabbah nimbly followed Tony across the traverse, and they continued with some urgency as October days are short and their planned bivouac site was still some distance above. The route now tackled a tricky diagonal ramp, but at its top the difficulty eased and they made good progress up the broad ridge that eventually led to the summit. The views were magnificent as the sun set behind distant storm-clouds, casting long black shadows on the desert floor far below and painting the sandstone fire red. As the light faded the trio were silhouetted against the westerly sky as they hurried upwards to their place of shelter.

The three climbers descend Jebel Rum by following Hammad's Route. Wadi Rum lies far below.

The bivouac site was perfect: a small *siq* with a soft sand floor, plenty of dead wood for a fire, and surrounding rock walls providing shelter from the cool night wind. With no inhibitions about wasting wood Sabbah soon had a roaring fire burning. He sat cross-legged, his deeply lined face highlighted by the dancing flames. As he waited for the water to boil he sang Bedouin love-songs in a soft alto voice that contrasted completely with his rugged appearance. A simple meal of chapatis, soup and sickly sweet Bedouin tea followed.

Next morning it took an hour of easy climbing over the rounded dome ridge to reach the summit. The view was breathtaking. The deep, flat-floored valleys between vertical rock towers formed a grid spreading in all directions, while far to the south the more pointed hills of the Saudi border rose through the heat-haze. To the north and west the expanse of desert was vast, and in the distance could just be made out occasional settlements near the Amman to Aqaba road. Unfortunately, this remote summit was spoilt by graffiti carved and painted on the rocks, and for such a rarely visited place a large amount of litter had been thrown down nearby cracks in the rock by visiting picknickers who arrived by helicopter!

Tony expressed disgust: 'Is nowhere sacred?' Elated by the summit, but disappointed by fellow man, they started the tortuous descent.

Complex route-finding is a feature of the Bedouin climbs, and this was highlighted as the descent constantly changed direction – over rock domes, traversing ledges, descending steep slabs and squeezing through narrow *siqs* just wide enough for a body. The terrain resembled a chaotic rock glacier. There was no track – occasional cairns marked the way – and if they blinked they could easily miss the route. Nowhere was it difficult enough to need to use a rope, and Sabbah strode out effortlessly in front with Tony and Di hurrying behind in an attempt to keep up. It was hot, thirsty work, and soon their meagre supplies of water ran out. Far below, the tiny model-like village of Wadi Rum beckoned.

After a couple of hours the huge gash of the Great Siq blocked their progress. This impressive *siq* cuts through Jebel Rum from east to west and provides a landmark for both Bedouin and climber, its 330-foot (100-m) vertical side walls requiring at least three exposed abseils before climbers can reach the cool, dark depths of its narrow, twisting bed. During storms this *siq* turns into a raging torrent in minutes as the run-off from the surrounding mountain is channelled into it. Today the sky

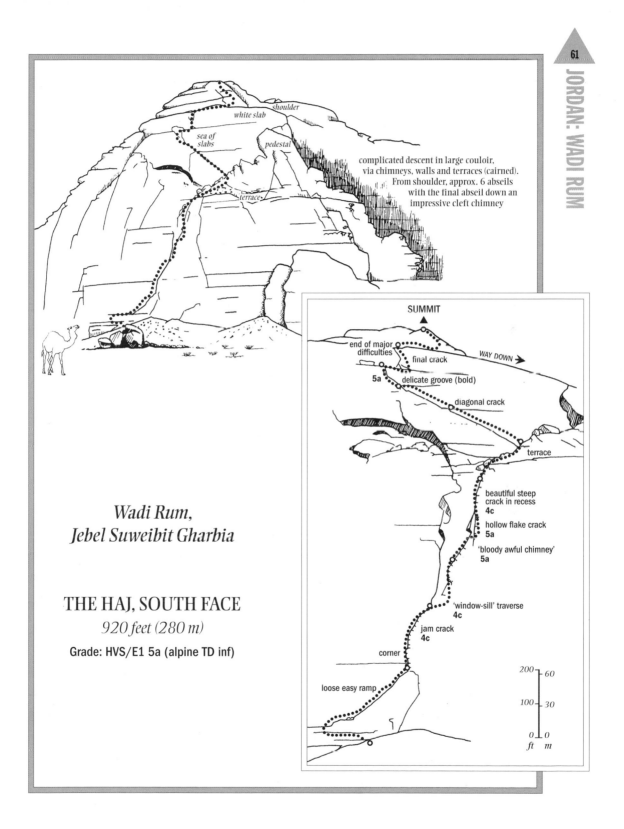

complicated descent in large couloir,
via chimneys, walls and terraces (cairned).
From shoulder, approx. 6 abseils
with the final abseil down an
impressive cleft chimney

shoulder

white slab

sea of
slabs

pedestal

terrace

*Wadi Rum,
Jebel Suweibit Gharbia*

THE HAJ, SOUTH FACE
920 feet (280 m)

Grade: HVS/E1 5a (alpine TD inf)

SUMMIT

end of major
difficulties
final crack

WAY DOWN

5a
delicate groove (bold)

diagonal crack

terrace

beautiful steep
crack in recess
4c

hollow flake crack
5a

'bloody awful chimney'
5a

'window-sill' traverse
4c

jam crack
4c

corner

loose easy ramp

200 — 60

100 — 30

0 — 0
ft   m

was clear, and Tony soon identified the lone tree around which they attached their abseil rope. Every footstep echoed as Tony concentrated on descending the sinister black water-polished walls to the sandy bed. Di and Sabbah soon joined him, and as they looked up to retrieve their ropes they could see only a narrow slit of blue sky far above. It felt more like caving than climbing! The *siq* was then descended by a series of dry water-holes carved beautifully in the soft rock. They emerged into sunlight as the *siq* steepened and then fell almost 1000 feet (305 m) through vertical cliffs. Fortuitously a rocky ridge snaked downwards to the right. At first this involved straightforward scrambling, but then it steepened and the trio were forced to make another abseil before reaching the valley screes.

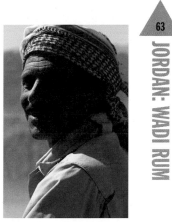

Sabbah Atieeq, the most experienced climber among the Bedouin and Tony's and Di's long-time friend.

With the descent finished but still overshadowed by the towering rock walls, they followed an intermittent track to a place where a small spring of cold, crystal-clear water gushed from the rocks and where lush herbs and green bushes created an exquisite oasis. The bird-song, bright green foliage and pungent mint assaulted their senses as they rested and quenched their thirst in this beautiful glade. Just below, the noise of a tourist group massing at Lawrence's Well disturbed their peace and reminded them of their return to civilization. They arose and soon reached the visitors at this once-beautiful well, now strewn with litter and carved with graffiti, before descending the path to the village of Wadi Rum.

It is a measure of the affection in which Tony and Di are held by the Bedouin that they were invited to join Sabbah's family for a traditional celebration, or *mensef*, that evening. Tony and Di have always been open in their dealings with his people and are particularly respectful of their customs. Consequently they have been welcomed as members of many local families. This feast was an opportunity not just to sample traditional food but also to exchange news and gossip. Contrary to Western tradition the preparations for the meal, the conversation and freshly

Sabbah abseils into the impressive Great Siq. This is the most spectacular section of the descent off Jebel Rum and in a storm can fill with a dangerous raging torrent within minutes.

ground coffee with which you are welcomed can take considerable time, but once the food is eaten everyone gets up somewhat abruptly and leaves.

After arriving, Di went across to the women's tents and spoke at length to a number of her friends, while Tony followed accepted custom and joined Sheikh Atieeq and the other men in the main tent. During the afternoon two sheep were ritually slaughtered and, some hours later, in the early evening two enormous silver plates were brought in, placed on old car tyres, and, by the light of the camp-fire and a solitary oil-lamp, the feast began.

Much of the attraction of such an event is in the little-observed details, be they the rhythmic grinding of coffee-beans by hand using a brass mortar and pestle or seeing the boiled sheep's head set right in the centre of each dish. As always, food is taken only with the right hand, and, following age-old practice, virtually every single part of the animal will have been cooked. Sometimes the Bedouin, who have a well-developed sense of humour, will mischievously watch reactions when particularly unusual morsels are handed around the circle of guests.

The morning after the *mensef*, Tony and Di set off to attempt their second climb. They drove in the Land Cruiser for two hours before they reached the remote solitude of the area along the old pilgrimage route to Mecca around Jebel Suweibit, which they had first explored with their friend and fellow desert fanatic Mick Shaw in 1995. Only the Bedouin normally venture this far south from Wadi Rum, and the hills marking the Saudi border could be seen clearly through the haze of the hot desert floor. The mountains were unusually beautiful even by Jordan's standards: mystical canyons cutting through 2000-foot (610-m) peaks with amazing rock architecture reminiscent of dripping candle-wax, tier after tier of huge rock formations resembling vivid red cauliflowers, walls peppered with thousands of caves like a giant Swiss cheese, and buttresses jutting forth as great bows of fossilized cruise liners.

After the bumpy, dusty and uncomfortable drive they pulled in to a small canyon near the base of an impressive rock face they had discovered and climbed on their first visit, naming it the Haj. They erected their tents in the shade of towering cliffs, sharing shelter from the sandstorms that can rise in an instant with a herd of 30 camels.

Next morning a half-hour walk took them to the base of the Haj. The 1000-foot (305-m) black and red sandstone face shone like polished wax. At its base lay scree and large boulders cleaved from the face by past geological events. The cliff was divided in two by a terrace at mid-height, and this gave the climb two different characters. The first half looked steep and strenuous, with the only possibility of success via a series of well-defined cracks and chimneys. Above the terrace the angle of the rock eased, and, although there were cracks at the start of the slab, near the top there was little in the way of features to climb. The outcome looked very uncertain indeed.

The approach pitch was easy enough though a bit loose, taking them into a cave at the bottom of the crack line. From there the climbing began in earnest.

They carefully negotiated the overhangs where the rock was a little doubtful, as desert sandstone often is, but once into the crack above they found brilliant middle-grade climbing. The crack soared skywards for about 100 feet (30 m) with no sign of a ledge to rest on and belay. It was great climbing all the way, laybacking, then jamming in a superb position with the vertical left wall above and the right wall swooping away to the scree below. The sun was full on the south face now, and the temperature began to soar.

Above, the crack steepened and the climbing in front looked difficult. The impasse was solved by a tiny horizontal ledge, no wider than a window-sill, leading right. With nose pressed against rock and not a handhold for help, Tony edged his way delicately towards a second, more amenable crack line. Almost as if by design the ledge widened as it reached the crack, providing a good belay to bring Di safely up. Higher, the crack steepened and widened and they were brought to an abrupt halt by 'the bloody awful chimney'!

Climbing is a perverse pursuit, and sometimes climbers have to suffer pain and terror to succeed. Many characterize it as stupid, masochistic and foolhardy, others as involving courage, mind over matter and rare determination to succeed against all odds. More often than not the body goes into automatic and a focus is achieved, probably a mixture of primitive instinct and a surge of adrenalin combined with years of training and experience. Tony was not one for psychoanalysis as he reached the top of the chimney, eyes bulging, dry-mouthed and gasping for breath. All that mattered was that he had succeeded and 'the bloody awful chimney' was a memory.

But they were not on safe ground yet. Above, they moved gingerly into a vertical crack, conscious that there was no room for error because their belay was poor and any fall would almost certainly have plunged them to certain death 600 feet (183 m) below. To make matters worse, the crack ascended several large hollow flakes that, alarmingly, appeared totally detached. As they climbed, the flakes moved and groaned as though the act of climbing would lever the 100-tonne slabs away from the main face. To leave the climb safer for others to follow, Di, being last up, pulled the largest flakes off and watched them spiralling into space and finally obliterating into a cloud of red dust as they hit the scree far below. Not before time a solid ledge marked the end of danger.

Above was a large rectangular recess, the left-hand corner of which gave the pair a marvellous pitch of middle-grade laybacking, jamming and bridging, a welcome contrast with the effort and terror of the chimney and flake below. At the top of the recess the angle suddenly eased and they were at the half-way ledge. They had succeeded on the bottom wall – but above lay the smooth upper slab.

Tony climbs the last easy slabs to the summit of the Haj. His hat is essential headgear to protect against the desert sun and the rucksack is used to carry water and emergency equipment.

Di started up a diagonal crack, the only weakness in the upper slab. Climbing quickly and confidently, she found it easier than expected. After another, slightly harder pitch they reached a worrying position, hanging from a poor belay on a small ledge with 800 feet (244 m) of space beneath their feet. Above, the rock was devoid of holds and Tony recalls it vividly:

I went up about 15 feet (4½ m) and there was a little natural hole through the rock which I managed to thread a five-millimetre cord through, and that, basically, was all my protection. Much better than nothing, but only as good as the fragile rock. From there I had to go for it, as I couldn't see any ledges above – nothing. I aimed for a patch of light-coloured rock about 20 feet (6 m) above, where there were obvious holds visible. The next section was the crux, and as I started to climb I was conscious of the rope snaking down to Di, holding it in case I fell. She shouted encouragement but was secretly apprehensive that the belay might fail if I slipped.

I kept thinking: It's all right – positive – really good friction, and it was quite a relief to start climbing after all the anxiety. I balanced up on rock which at first looked too steep to climb without footholds. My rock boots padded on the smooth sandstone. At first some finger pockets were a help, but then it became blank. I kept trying to move diagonally right to where the weakness of the rock suggested, but as I tried the moves it felt wrong and I had to teeter down. I searched for a long time, trying to read the rock and solve the puzzle. It was a mind game, like vertical chess up there, not like the brawn of the chimney below. One half of the mind thinking of the dangerous fall if I blew it, the other half pushing me on, convincing me of my ability. Eventually, I looked left, and hidden around the side of a small nose of rock was the key, a small but good foothold. A quick step up and I was on easier-angled rock.

The final pitch to the top was easy by comparison. Hands reached for warm sandstone, feet ran up easy-angled rock with thousands of feet of space below. On the summit, as evening shadows turned the desert floor blue, they felt fulfilment and an inner feeling of satisfaction.

On the long journey back to Wadi Rum the next day, however, Tony and Di were full of mixed emotions. When they first came here they found a region that had been virtually unaffected by modern tourism. At that time the Bedouin lived in their time-honoured nomadic way, but the intervening years have seen profound changes to that traditional lifestyle and Tony and Di are now deeply concerned for its continuation. As Tony explains:

> Today there is a lot more tourism. The borders with Israel have opened up, and Wadi Rum itself is extremely busy. People are also coming up from the big cities like Aqaba and Amman. They drive all over the desert and destroy the ecologically fragile surface and vegetation. Quite recently trees have been chopped down to make barbecues and picnics. Another tour group painted blue arrows up one of the famous Bedouin climbs so they and their clients wouldn't get lost.

Faced with a threat to an area they felt so committed to, Tony and Di have approached Jordan's Royal Family, in particular Queen Noor (who is patron of Jordan's Royal Society for the Conservation of Nature), and joined other conservation groups in order to protect one of the country's most valuable environments.

Tony has a clear view of how he would like to see Wadi Rum develop and has discussed the matter with Sabbah and his fellow Bedouin.

> We are now working to try and create a national park, which is a totally new concept. At first the Bedouin had no real idea what a national park was but, having explained it to them, they suddenly see in the last two or three years that things really are changing fast. There is even a threat to remove the village and push all the Bedouin outside the area, 10 miles (16 km) down the road, and build big hotels there.
>
> They have contacted King Hussein directly about this because, as I understand it, he gave them the right to live in the valley. I think the king is supporting them, but we are fighting very hard to make sure that they continue to live in the area and have a major say in what happens to it.

RECOMMENDED ROUTES

Tony and Di suggest that a climbing holiday should start with a walk through Rakabat Canyon and while there do either Essence of Rum or The Beauty, depending on ability.

If confident of route-finding go up Jebel Rum via Sheikh Hamdan's or Sabbah's Route and down Hammad's Route. If not confident, then go up and down Hammad's Route. Bigger and more serious climbs are the classics of Pillar of Wisdom, Inshallah Factor, Lionheart and Muezzin.

A great trip is to go out to Barrah Canyon and spend the night there. In the canyon are many fantastic climbs, with Merlin's Wand, a 500-foot (150-m) crack, the pick of the bunch.

It is well worth making the effort to visit some of the more remote areas such as Burdah (with its now famous rock bridge), where Orange Sunshine is superb. Alternatively, try Al Uzza on Jebel Khazali or, if you are feeling particularly adventurous, visit the Haj.

Asked if a national park is a realistic proposition, Tony is less sure. Not because of the attitude of the Bedouin but of those elsewhere in the country. 'They have suddenly realized that Wadi Rum is a big money-earner so it is very difficult to say. At the moment it is in the lap of the gods.'

For both Tony and Di the climbs remain as fine as ever and new lines are still to be discovered, but they both feel inextricably linked to the future of this community. Within a week they will be back home, sending faxes to conservation bodies, the Ministry of Tourism and even Queen Noor herself. They came to this area to climb and to enjoy the hospitality of the Bedouin but, like T. E. Lawrence over half a century earlier, they are now umbilically bound to the people and their future.

Barry Blanchard and Nancy Feagin

The Cirque of the Unclimbables, Canada

3

The lightning flashes split the sky into irregular blocks of ominous grey and black and the torrential downpour, more reminiscent of equatorial Africa than subarctic Canada, forced water on to every part of the body, but most impressive of all was the thunder. It built up suddenly to a loud growl that reverberated around the encircling mountains for many seconds until it eventually faded away, leaving just the sound of wind and rain. After a journey through one of the least inhabited landscapes outside Antarctica, Barry Blanchard and Nancy Feagin had arrived in the Cirque of the Unclimbables.

Today, despite being accorded a place of honour in Roper and Steck's *Fifty Classic Climbs of North America*, and hence on the wish-list of many ambitious climbers, the Cirque remains remote and, in comparison with many of the world's

Nancy Feagin and Barry Blanchard 'hanging out' on a belay half-way up the south-east face of Proboscis. To climb such a big wall requires a lot of rope and equipment.

other mountain ranges, relatively unvisited. With better access it would draw hundreds of climbers from around the world for on its smooth granite faces lie not only some extraordinarily demanding routes but a whole host of unclimbed lines that offer tremendous potential for future first ascents. It was the possibility of making an ascent of the dramatic south-east face of Proboscis that tempted Nancy

THE CIRQUE'S CLIMBING HISTORY

The Cirque lies at the northern tip of the Logan Mountains, and it was Arnold Wexler, a member of the 1955 expedition to these mountains, who was the first person to describe the area in detail and climb some of the easier peaks. However, he assessed that most of the peaks would be unclimbable, a pronouncement that soon caught the attention of the mountaineering community.

In 1960 a young mountaineer called Bill Buckingham, who had climbed extensively in the Tetons and Bugaboos, organized an expedition to the newly christened 'Cirque of the Unclimbables'. Over a period of a month, his team succeeded on nearly every high point in the Cirque, usually by intricate and devious routes that bypassed the major walls. Their greatest success was the first ascent of Proboscis by the south ridge. Although the high points had been reached, the main walls remained unclimbed, awaiting a new breed of climber with the skills to succeed on the vertical granite. In 1963 Proboscis was again the centre of attention when McCarthy, Kor, Robbins and McCracken used Yosemite big wall techniques to climb the south-east face.

The striking 2000-foot (610-m) south-east buttress of Lotus Flower Tower was next to attract the attention of Yosemite climbers. In 1968 J. McCarthy, T. Frost and S. Bill pioneered a route up this beautiful prow of granite. This route was climbed free in 1977 and is deservedly the most popular climb in the Cirque.

Big wall-climbing became increasingly popular throughout the 1970s, reaching its peak in 1977 with many walls being climbed for the first time. After this, most expeditions arrived to climb Lotus Flower Tower. That was until 1992, when Skinner, Piana and Rowell brought Proboscis back into the limelight with their ground-breaking ascent of The Great Canadian Knife on the south-east face. Since then, further difficult ascents on this wall have kept it in the spotlight.

Feagin and Barry Blanchard to the Cirque, although, looking up at its high face running with water after the storm, their proposed ascent looked very ambitious: the size – over a third of a mile high – sheer inaccessibility and the fickle weather of the Cirque have a habit of defeating most climbers' plans. Just getting here is an expedition in itself. The flight from Fort Simpson in the Twin Otter took over an hour, and when it gently feathered the inky blue waters of Glacier Lake on touch-down, it seemed a stark intrusion in a wild habitat whose most striking occupant is the grizzly bear.

The journey to the Cirque in the Logan Mountains was a gradual transition from the modern world to a vast wilderness that has been almost entirely unaltered by the course of human history. It began in Yellowknife, a community grandly called the capital of Canada's Northwest Territories but in reality a small town of 19,000 people and the last opportunity to buy any specialist gear before heading north-west. The scale of this landscape can be gleaned from just a few statistics: the Northwest Territories cover an area of more than half a million square miles (1.3 million sq km) – equivalent, in fact, to France, Germany and Spain combined – yet is home to only 100,000 people. It contains two inland seas (including the Great Slave Lake on whose north-western shores Yellowknife was founded) but the land itself is one of rock

and trees. One of North America's last great wildlife refuges, it contains literally hundreds of peaks that have never felt a human footfall on them.

The flight in to Yellowknife descends over a stunning archipelago surrounding the shores of the Great Slave Lake which, if it looks like anywhere else, most closely resembles the wildest parts of Scandinavia. Yet this was only the start of the journey. The jumping-off point for the Cirque lay some 360 miles (580 km) away at Fort Simpson, a journey that takes only an hour by air but all day by road, despite passing through only three small communities. It involved ferry crossings

The massive 2000-foot (610-m) south-east face of Proboscis. The mountain is one of the hardest to climb in North America and received its first ascent via Contact Peak (the left-hand peak), then the saw-toothed skyline ridge to the summit at the right-hand side. The Original Route on the face roughly follows the stepped corners to the right of the large corner system in the centre of the photograph.

of the massive Mackenzie and Liard rivers (everything in Canada seems painted on a larger canvas), with Barry and Nancy travelling along mile after mile of deserted dirt roads and passing through innumerable acres of forest and muskeg. There can be few better introductions to the Canadian north country than this journey under vast, panoramic skies where even the few scattered communities were less significant than their names suggested. Looking across the vast wilderness and remembering that the native peoples had the skills to live, hunt and travel throughout such inhospitable terrain put their remarkable achievements in true perspective. In the Northwest Territories there are nine official languages and nine separate cultural groups, all of whom retain their own identity: the main groups around Fort Simpson are the Dene and the Métis. They either live within the Fort Simpson community itself or come there from even smaller settlements to shop, get medical attention or attend school.

These aboriginals sometimes view themselves as the real Northerners, but today they have been joined by an eclectic collection of people who service this frontier village, and the individual characters, many visiting from remote outposts in the bush, are an assorted bunch displaying a variety of accents, hairstyles and clothing. Fans of the Channel 4 series *Northern Exposure* would feel immediately at home. In the bad weather that can dog the Cirque, it is not uncommon for groups to get stranded here: such an occurrence offers an opportunity to explore the community and also to gain closer acquaintance with what Barry termed the 'pit bull mosquitoes and Rottweiler horseflies'.

Rafting and fishing are the main tourist attractions, but even here the numbers are small, with only 2400 estimated visitors making the long journey up to Fort Simpson each year. From here the final leg of the journey into the Cirque was by float plane to Glacier Lake and, by common consent, undoubtedly the most spectacular. Taking off from the Mackenzie River itself was an unforgettable experience, especially as the Twin Otter was heavily laden, and the hour-and-a-half flight includes an aerial perspective of the South Nahanni River snaking its majestic way through this empty landscape and of dozens of smaller summits that line the route.

The pilot, Jacques Harvey, was hugely experienced in operating in this region and on the way in gave Barry and Nancy a dramatic close-up of their proposed route on Proboscis followed by a sharp turn to port as the wall appeared ominously close. It was a scene reminiscent of countless war movies but had provided an eagle's-eye view of the face. Within seconds there followed a rapid descent and a velvet landing on Glacier Lake, some 7000 feet (2135 m) below, just as the electric storm blew in. Finally, with the help of another very experienced pilot, Jim Broadbent, all the climbing gear, food and other equipment was lifted by helicopter to base camp.

After almost three days of continuous travelling, Barry Blanchard and Nancy Feagin had the first opportunity to take stock of their new surroundings. For many years Barry Blanchard has been one of Canada's top alpinists. Although he has made many notable ascents throughout the country, this was his first visit to the Cirque and his facial expressions showed that he was clearly savouring every moment.

Barry has a strong, powerful build, but it is his wide, mischievous eyes, an enormous sense of humour (his vocal imitations of characters from *The Simpsons*, especially Homer, are uncannily accurate) and his giant personality that attract the attention. Now 38, but managing to look both younger and older at the same time, he is of Métis descent and this background of French Canadian and American Indian has been increasingly important to him in recent years. He is immensely proud to be Canadian and is particularly attracted to the wilder parts of his country. He specializes in alpine ice-climbing and has made successful ascents of many Canadian classics, including routes on McKinley, Kitchener and Temple. In 1985 he ascended the North Pillar of North Twin in the company of the late Dave Cheesmond, and in doing so they established a line that for many years was thought of as the hardest alpine route in North America. Barry has also made a number of trips to the Himalayas. In 1993 he attempted that most dangerous of mountains, K2, but turned back at around 26,000 feet (8000 m) when he felt insufficiently in control and with worsening weather in prospect. All six climbers ahead of Barry and his partner at the 'bottleneck' on K2's shoulder managed to reach the summit but, of those six, half died descending from the top when the storm broke. In Barry's words, 'gone forever'. Similarly bad weather also defeated their attempts at the summit on Nanga Parbat, and on

WEATHER AND SEASONS

Late June to the end of August is the best time to visit the Cirque. Deep snow can be encountered into June and torrential rain occurs frequently throughout the summer. Occasional cold spells can bring snow to the summits and sometimes down to the tree line. Fortunately, spells of excellent weather often last up to five days, during which temperatures can reach the low 20s °C. The downside of good weather are the swarms of mosquitoes which plague base camp. Twenty-four-hour daylight in June and very long days in July and August allow one to take maximum advantage of good weather. September brings shorter days, colder conditions and snow which lingers on the faces.

Everest altitude sickness and later exhaustion forced a retreat. Yet Barry can be a bold climber as well as a prudent one and his first Himalayan expedition concluded with a last-minute ascent of Rakaposhi, where he briefly stood on the summit despite an electric storm.

Today Barry is partner to Catherine (his second marriage), who worked previously in publishing and television, and his easygoing manner and casual appearance do much to mask a life that has had more than its fair share of pain. Behind the long mane of greying hair and chipped-tooth grin, Barry has experienced climbing's darker side and has been forced to decide whether the gains can ever compensate for the risks and losses involved. During the mid-1980s he had to confront a series of tragic accidents that heralded a protracted dark period in his life. Faced with a succession of deeply painful experiences, Barry doubted his own ability to continue climbing in the face of such overwhelming tragedy.

These events began in 1986 when a group of four students – two male, two female – he was teaching had an accident while descending a snow slope. Their initial fall probably would not have been so serious had it not triggered an avalanche that engulfed two of the party and also Barry. He made swimming motions as he was dragged beneath the wet snow and fortunately managed to extricate himself. He searched frantically and discovered that two members of his party had been similarly buried. Although they were found and dug out after a short while, both had stopped breathing and, even worse, both failed to respond to all Barry's attempts at reviving them and died. While there will always be an element of risk in the mountains, Barry, as the instructor to these novice climbers, felt an enormous responsibility for their safety. In the aftermath of the accident he gave up guiding for a while as he tried to come to terms with their deaths.

Within months more fundamental questions were raised about the risk game when two close friends died in Alaska but the final blow came with the death of Dave Cheesmond who was killed on Mount Logan in the Yukon. The two had an exceptionally close relationship spanning five years at a crucial stage in Barry's life. After months of intense introspection Barry came to realize that his relationship with Cheesmond had been founded on their mutual love of climbing and the many great routes they had undertaken together. Like other climbers in similar

Nancy's and Barry's lives are committed to climbing but they specialize in different aspects of the sport: Barry favours mountaineering, especially on alpine ice faces, whereas Nancy prefers hard-rock climbing.

situations, he worked out that both Cheesmond's life and his own had been defined by climbing. Without the risk, the adventure and even the pain, they would be quite different people. What followed was a long, painful coming to terms with both Cheesmond's death and that of other friends – and a gradual return to climbing.

Nancy Feagin teamed up with Barry on this trip to the Cirque of the Unclimbables. Unlike fellow Canadian climbers with whom Barry had built up strong relationships, he and Nancy knew of each other only by reputation. However, when this climb was first suggested, Nancy made a winter visit to Barry's home in Canmore, Alberta. The pair went off in search of ice-climbs and came back with a respect for each other's ability and the seeds of a new friendship. Some seven years younger than Barry, Nancy is a petite 5 feet 2 inches (1.57 m) who was brought up in Jackson, Wyoming, but who now lives in Salt Lake City. Nancy has been climbing since her teens, and originally she was best known in the States for her competition climbing. Yet to think of her as such gives a vastly misleading impression, for she is interested in all aspects of climbing and has recently spent much time tackling long routes on big walls. Her climbing achievements are impressive. For example, she has climbed extensively in Yosemite and was a member of the team who free-climbed the direct north-west route on Half Dome. Also in Yosemite, she has made one-day ascents of Salathé Wall and The Nose. Nancy has achieved a number of solo ascents in Zion National Park, Utah, including such lines as Sheer Lunacy, Touchstone Wall, Space Shot and Moonlight Buttress. She has also climbed in the Grand Tetons and Wind Rivers and has been active in Alaska, Mexico, Patagonia and Argentina in addition to Canada. Unlike Barry who had never previously visited the Cirque, Nancy came here in 1995 with Doug Heinrich to climb Lotus Flower Tower.

Now 31, Nancy is distinguished by her devastating smile and electric-blue eyes and by one other attribute – she simply does not give up. She has a determination that is almost in inverse proportion to her size and gives the impression that she will not be beaten until her reserves of energy are exhausted. She loves to chat away on a route and is fascinated by the technical difficulties posed by it. She learnt to climb while at school in Jackson after signing up for a course with her mother. Both had been fascinated by the majestic peaks of the Tetons, but for Nancy this introduction to climbing was a revelation. She took a traditional career path through university, where she earned not one but two degrees in the usual four-year period. Qualified in electrical engineering and computer science, Nancy got work as a writer of computer software, but after three years' travel, climbing held more attraction than a regular pay cheque and she left the office one Friday in 1990 for a climbing trip in South America and never returned.

The brief helicopter uplift from Glacier Lake used by Barry and Nancy was the painless way into the Cirque. It saves a day carrying in each load to the Fairy Meadows base camp for climbers attempting routes on Lotus Flower Tower, but for lines on Proboscis the savings are even greater. On foot the route would take two laborious days via Fairy Meadows and then over a col called What Notch to find a camp beneath the wall of Proboscis. In the earlier part of the season this can still be covered with snow and ice and, although not technically demanding, would require care and be a hard slog with heavy packs.

Once the noise of the helicopter had abated, Nancy and Barry were left gazing, transfixed, at the majestic face of Proboscis in full view of their base camp, admiring its clean lines with a series of expressive gasps and sighs. Around and above them sheer amphitheatres of rock rose dramatically. The Cirque of the Unclimbables was certainly an apt name for this remote mountain range from which it would take about two weeks to reach the nearest community if you had to hike out. As Barry reflected, this was an 'awesomely remote place'.

At breakfast on 5 July, the first morning at base camp, there was a strange mixture of emotions: tiredness, understandable after the long and complex journey followed by the mad rush to erect a camp in the storm the evening before; a sense of unreality, which often occurs when planes and helicopters land adventurers in remote places only to disappear, severing the thread with the modern world; and finally impatience or perhaps a keen desire to get to grips with the climb, highlighted as the bad weather had cleared and now there was a cloudless sky.

A storm clears as the helicopter ferries loads from Glacier Lake to base camp in the heart of the Cirque of the Unclimbables. A ten-minute flight instead of a two-day walk!

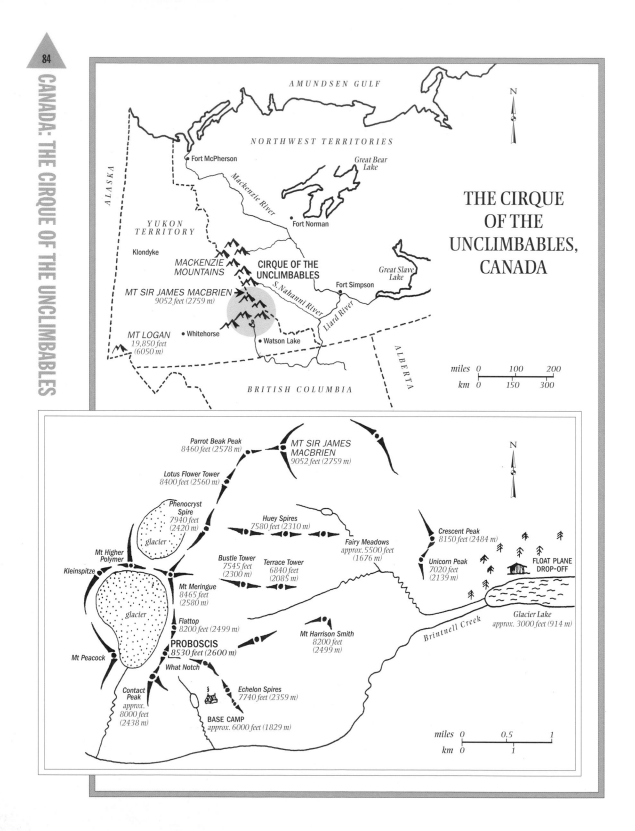

THE CIRQUE
OF THE
UNCLIMBABLES,
CANADA

AMUNDSEN GULF

N

NORTHWEST TERRITORIES

Fort McPherson

Great Bear
Lake

ALASKA

Mackenzie River

YUKON
TERRITORY

Fort Norman

Klondyke

MACKENZIE
MOUNTAINS

CIRQUE OF THE
UNCLIMBABLES

Great Slave
Lake

MT SIR JAMES MACBRIEN
9052 feet (2759 m)

Fort Simpson

S. Nahanni River

Liard River

MT LOGAN
19,850 feet
(6050 m)

Whitehorse

Watson Lake

ALBERTA

BRITISH COLUMBIA

miles 0   100   200
km   0   150   300

Parrot Beak Peak
8460 feet (2578 m)

MT SIR JAMES
MACBRIEN
9052 feet (2759 m)

N

Lotus Flower Tower
8400 feet (2560 m)

Phenocryst
Spire
7940 feet
(2420 m)

glacier

Huey Spires
7580 feet (2310 m)

Crescent Peak
8150 feet (2484 m)

Fairy Meadows
approx. 5500 feet
(1676 m)

Mt Higher
Polymer

Kleinspitze

Bustle Tower
7545 feet
(2300 m)

Terrace Tower
6840 feet
(2085 m)

Unicorn Peak
7020 feet
(2139 m)

FLOAT PLANE
DROP-OFF

glacier

Mt Meringue
8465 feet
(2580 m)

Flattop
8200 feet (2499 m)

PROBOSCIS
8530 feet (2600 m)

Mt Harrison Smith
8200 feet
(2499 m)

Brintnell Creek

Glacier Lake
approx. 3000 feet (914 m)

Mt Peacock

What Notch

Contact
Peak
approx.
8000 feet
(2438 m)

Echelon Spires
7740 feet (2359 m)

BASE CAMP
approx. 6000 feet (1829 m)

miles 0   0.5   1
km   0   1

Barry and Nancy had planned to spend the first couple of days unpacking and sorting out their half-tonne of food, climbing gear and camping kit. With the fine weather all this had to change. They knew the area's reputation for depressingly wet weather. Climbing teams had been known to visit the area for three weeks and depart without seeing their objective due to low cloud and rain. Nancy's 1995 success on nearby Lotus Flower Tower had been achieved in two days of rare fine weather when the almost 24-hour daylight, which occurs at these high latitudes in midsummer, enabled them to complete their objective in an intense and exhausting burst of round-the-clock climbing .

'We must start climbing today,' Nancy implored Barry, then added: 'This may be the only good weather spell we get in our two weeks!' Barry, still trying to kick-start his body with his third cup of coffee, was more fatalistic. 'Yeah, mmm. All we can do is try the route. If the weather's good, so be it.'

There are no set rules by which these difficult and high, remote alpine rock faces are climbed, but Barry and Nancy, who are at the cutting edge of the sport, would try to follow what is considered the best ethic or practice of the day. Conversely, due to their position within the sport they are also opinion-formers and the methods employed while climbing Proboscis would be followed keenly by their peer group. They had to choose carefully how or in what style to climb such a face, considering the weather, difficulty and length of climb.

Nancy summed up her own views on ethics: 'I try to strive for the purest possible style of ascent, but everybody is out there to satisfy their own goals and as long as this is reported accurately then that's OK by me.'

Until the middle of this century an ascent of the south-east face of Proboscis would have been virtually impossible. It was not until the 1950s that climbers gained sufficient expertise and invented special equipment (particularly hard steel pitons used for artificial aid) to attempt such difficult faces and begin what has been christened big wall-climbing. Then parallel but separate developments in Europe and the United States produced a series of remarkable ascents typified by the famous Italian climber Walter Bonatti's solo ascent in 1955 of the south-west pillar of the Petit Dru in the French Alps and a team led by Warren Harding climbing The Nose on El Capitan in the Yosemite Valley, California, in 1958.

When in 1963 James P. McCarthy, Layton Kor, Richard McCracken and Royal Robbins made the long journey north from California to the Cirque to attempt Proboscis, they brought with them knowledge gained from a series of exceptionally difficult ascents in Yosemite. They completed the climb in what has been called their three-day blitz, during which they used over 250 pitons for artificial aid. The climb heralded a new era as technically difficult big wall-climbing methods were applied in an isolated alpine environment. Interestingly, after the ascent they compared the south-east face of Proboscis with the north-west face of Half Dome in Yosemite, which Robbins had made the first ascent of six years earlier, but whereas the scale was the same, the Yukon weather was somewhat different from that found in California.

Nancy was very impressed by this ascent of Proboscis. 'They were amazing climbers for their time, considering their hawser ropes, shoes and gear, with no cams – and to do it in three days! It's still the most logical and aesthetic route on the face.'

From base camp the full grandeur of the face stood bastion at the end of a high valley. Through binoculars they could pick out the various routes that had been made on the mountain. An easy broken ridge of loose red rock on the left (south) of the face gave access by scrambling and easy climbing to a sub-summit called Contact Peak, from which, after a small col, the almost horizontal, saw-toothed ridge led to the summit, at 8530 feet (2600 m) on which remnants of winter snow still clung. A party led by Bill Buckingham made the first ascent of the peak in 1960 and found it one of the hardest rock peaks in North America with difficult climbing which they graded IV 5.7 A2. Looking into the future, Barry and Nancy optimistically identified Buckingham's ascent route as a possible descent of the mountain – if they ever managed to reach the summit!

Below the southern ridge the south-east face dropped sheer to the scree 2000 feet (610 m) below. This mile-wide, yellow monolithic slab, stained black and grey by water streaks from patches of snow on the summit, appeared feature-less from a distance, but through the binoculars Barry could make out crack lines, grooves, dihedrals and overhangs which identified the routes now climbing the face: from left to right Great Canadian Knife (first ascent in 1991), Yukon Tears (f.a. 1994), The Grendel (f.a. 1996), Original Route (f.a. 1963, with Spanish

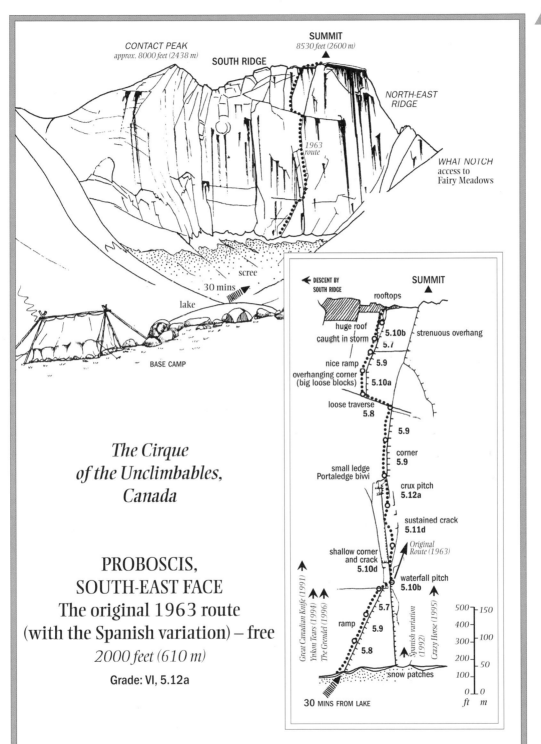

CONTACT PEAK
approx. 8000 feet (2438 m)

SUMMIT
8530 feet (2600 m)

SOUTH RIDGE

NORTH-EAST
RIDGE

WHAT NOTCH
access to
Fairy Meadows

1963
route

scree

30 mins

lake

BASE CAMP

*The Cirque
of the Unclimbables,
Canada*

**PROBOSCIS,
SOUTH-EAST FACE**
The original 1963 route
(with the Spanish variation) – free
2000 feet (610 m)

Grade: VI, 5.12a

DESCENT BY
SOUTH RIDGE

SUMMIT

rooftops

huge roof
caught in storm

5.10b   strenuous overhang

5.7

nice ramp   5.9

overhanging corner
(big loose blocks)   5.10a

loose traverse
5.8

5.9

corner
5.9

small ledge
Portaledge bivvi

crux pitch
5.12a

sustained crack
5.11d

*Original
Route (1963)*

shallow corner
and crack
5.10d

waterfall pitch
5.10b

5.7

ramp   5.9

5.8

*Spanish variation
(1992)*

snow patches

Great Canadian Knife (1991)
Yukon Tears (1994)
The Grendel (1996)

Crazy Horse (1995)

500 — 150
400
300 — 100
200 — 50
100
0 — 0
ft   m

30 MINS FROM LAKE

variation, Via Costa Brava, f.a. 1992) and The Spanish Route/Crazy Horse (f.a. 1995). Out of sight around the steep right-hand ridge the North-East Face Route (f.a. 1977) was the only other route to the summit.

The recent origin of these routes on the face confirmed to Nancy and Barry the difficulties they would encounter. Only Great Canadian Knife and Yukon Tears had been climbed free, and these were two of the hardest multi-pitch rock routes in the world, their first ascensionists being among the best climbers in the United States. The other climbs all had difficult artificial aid. Also, notably, apart from Original Route, the other routes had not been climbed in one push; rather 'siege tactics' had been used by climbing short (165- to 330-foot /50- to 100-m) sections of one or two pitches a day, then fixing a rope at their high points so the climbers could descend to the ground, then regain their high point the next day or when suitable weather allowed. This method, though not in the best style, allowed the brief spells of good weather to be utilized to the maximum, but completing the climb often took two or three weeks.

Now that Barry and Nancy had identified the climbs and features on the face, they could easily see that the most feasible and exciting challenge was to attempt the first free ascent of Original Route and clearly, they argued, to have any chance of success, siege tactics similar to those used on the other ascents would have to be adopted. They started sorting their gear with this plan in mind.

It was after midday before they left base camp and started the 1-mile (1.5-km), hour-long walk to the foot of the face. Large, car-sized boulders covered in slippery wet moss immediately slowed progress. Nancy took great care in placing her feet as she picked the best line through the giant scree, reminding herself how easy it would be to slip and turn an ankle or, worse, break a leg on such apparently benign terrain. Barry followed, placing small cairns to indicate the route for their return. Soon the boulder field ended, and they traversed on steep grass above a small glacial lake covered in cracked winter ice coloured blue-white. At the lake's edge the ice had melted, and in the calm indigo water they could see the reflection of Proboscis.

After a mile the grass gave way to moraine and patches of soft snow. It cannot have been many years ago that glaciers would have filled this valley, and the land-scape below the face was a legacy of a recent, colder age. A flat, cleared patch of moraine ten minutes below the face indicated the advanced base camp of past climbing parties and was a suitable place at which to stop and study their route.

'Pretty impressive, eh, Nancy?' Barry exclaimed, craning his neck backwards as his gaze took in the phenomenal slab of rock reaching skywards.

'Look over there. See where the snow cone is lying at the bottom. Original Route starts there and follows a ramp diagonally to the right, up to that wet patch,' Nancy replied excitedly, then asked: 'Have you got the binoculars, Barry?'

Nancy scanned the face, stopping intermittently to study the details. 'Oh, no, that wet patch is more like a waterfall and the cracks above are dripping. That should be fun!'

'Let me have a look,' said Barry. 'Look over there. You can see the belay bolts on The Knife and Yukon Tears.' Then he added: 'The rock looks fantastic. Let's go and have a closer look.'

They put their harnesses on and arranged their gear before scrambling up the scree, then waded through the soft, melting snow which still banked out from the bottom of the rock. At the junction with the rock they made a ledge in the snow and changed from their boots to their rock shoes and then tied into the rope. After all the travel and preparation they were finally ready to climb.

Barry started and made quick progress up the easy-angled rock of the ramp. 'The rock's warm but all the cracks are running with water,' he bellowed.

'What does it look like above?' Nancy shouted.

'Good. I'll be at the first belay soon,' Barry replied.

It took a couple of hours to climb three straightforward pitches before they reached the end of the ramp.

'Looks pretty wet to me and that traverse looks tricky,' Nancy said with some understatement.

To their right a holdless and unprotected horizontal traverse led to the bottom of a black, dank and unpleasant chimney down which a torrent of water gushed. On the following day they would return to their high point to battle with the waterfall pitch.

To descend, they tied their ropes together so they were long enough to reach the ground, then fixed them to the belay and abseiled to the base. They left the ropes in place so that they could reascend them to reach their high point tomorrow. Satisfied with the start they had made, they headed back to base.

That evening, as they discussed tactics, it became obvious that they needed to place a couple of bolts to protect the traverse into the waterfall then hope that the next wet section had plenty of holds so they could climb it without aid. They would also need a lot of rope carried to below the climb, ready to fix each pitch with rope as they progressed higher.

The following day was again fine but they had essential base camp chores to attend to before they could think of climbing. First they had to dig a toilet pit and then find the best source of water, hopefully not too near the pit! Food and gear had to be sorted and the kitchen tent erected, so it was not until early afternoon that Barry reached the bottom of the climb and carefully attached his two ascenders to the rope.

These mechanical devices are designed to help a person climb a rope; their special cams allow them to slide easily up the rope but, when weighted, they lock, preventing them from sliding down. One is attached to the waist harness, the other via a long sling to a foot loop. By alternately straightening the legs and then hanging from the waist, slow but steady progress is made up the rope. Climbing a rope in this fashion was a lot easier than climbing the rock, and Barry made quick progress up the rope they had left in place the day before. But it was a strenuous and laborious task, and Barry had to pause frequently to catch his breath.

When he reached their previous high point he pulled up a rucksack full of climbing gear and enough rope for fixing the next few pitches above. That Nancy followed quickly without stopping was perhaps indicative of the contrasting way they had spent the last month, Nancy rock-climbing on the big walls of Yosemite and Barry guiding clients up the snow slopes of the Cordillera Blanca in the Peruvian Andes.

It was a time-consuming business getting all the gear prepared, hanging on the belay over 300 feet (90 m) above the ground, and it was well into the evening before three bolts had been placed to protect the traverse into the waterfall. This was done by first drilling the rock with a battery-operated drill, a strenuous and precarious operation, then placing 0.4-inch (10-mm) diameter expansion bolts in the holes. This completed, it was time to descend the ropes and return to camp.

◀ Barry climbing the first steep pitch of the Spanish variation to the Original Route. Nancy is belaying and below her can be seen part of the notorious waterfall pitch, fortunately drier than when they first climbed it.

The morning of the third day was still fine and Nancy and Barry could not believe their good fortune, but at the same time they were worried by their slow progress. They had climbed three easy pitches out of the 15 they estimated it would take to get to the top and they had only eight more days left. Above, the climbing would get much harder. To have any chance of success they would have to make faster progress and be lucky with the weather.

Later in the day ominous high clouds filled the sky, and the nearby summits disappeared under a grey blanket. Despite the forbidding weather, Nancy started the difficult traverse. The problem was that where she wanted to place her feet there was a series of loose flakes that could break off easily if she stood on them. Instead, she had to teeter rightwards on small crystals in the granite. Unfortunately, as she got nearer the waterfall the spray wet the rock, making it very slippery. The bolts that had been placed the day before reduced the danger if she fell, but Nancy was still nervous. With skill she reached the chimney, but she was now under the full force of the waterfall. As she reached up for a hold, water poured into her cuff, down her back and out at her ankles, immediately soaking her to the skin despite her waterproofs.

The cold water was sapping heat and strength from Nancy and she had to move quickly through the torrent, yet everything was against her. Her hands were losing feeling, the rock was slippery and she could hardly look up against the deluge to find the holds. Barry, at first amused, became increasingly worried at her predicament and shouted encouragement. The really wet section was only 30 feet (9 m) long, and Nancy decided that her best option was to climb in short, rapid bursts and to rest to place protection and gain her composure. By bridging her feet across the chimney, she took most of the weight from her arms and, showing a fantastic display of skill, determination and gritty courage, eventually she pulled on to a ledge at the top of the chimney and came out of the firing line of the water.

While arranging the belay she realized that she had been so engrossed in the climbing that she had not noticed the rapid deterioration in the weather. Rain was starting to fall, and Barry was distinctly agitated on the belay below.

'On belay. Climb, Barry,' Nancy stuttered as she shivered uncontrollably.

'I'm on my way,' Barry shouted with a distinct lack of enthusiasm.

By the time he reached Nancy at the belay the rain was torrential, but it didn't really matter: looking like drowned rats, they could not get any wetter if they tried. However, it soon became a matter of urgency for them to evacuate before they became hypothermic. They were also anxious that the sheets of water now cascading down the face, as the intensity of the storm increased, could dislodge loose rocks above them. It is in such situations that experience counts; panic can easily lead to mistakes. Carefully and systematically they descended their fixed rope to the ground and made record time back to camp.

Rain fell constantly while they ate that evening. Water poured from the edge of the tarpaulin sheltering the eating area and what had once been a trickle of a stream passing through the campsite now became a foaming torrent, narrowly missing the tents. In the Cirque, weather like this often lasts weeks, not days. Would this bring their plans and efforts to a premature conclusion? With no weather forecast, they could only hope.

Fortuitously, the rain abated in the early hours and had cleared by 8 a.m., though a cold wind blew turbulent clouds across the sky. It took under an hour to reach the face, and by pulling the rope slightly to the left of the waterfall they managed to arrive at their high ledge relatively dry. Above, the route divided and a decision had to be made as to which way to go. To the right, Original Route followed a ramp with a crack in the back for 100 feet (30 m) before it petered out; from there a series of discontinuous thin cracks described a tenuous line for over 300 feet (91 m) to what appeared to be a small series of ledges. It was obvious why the first ascensionists had followed this line, as even after the heavy rain it was dry and the cracks were ideal for hammering in narrow pegs. Unfortunately, the steepness and the holdless nature of the rock made it extremely unlikely that Nancy or Barry would be able to free-climb this section. However, directly above was a single wide crack that cleaved the granite wall for 450 feet (137 m). This had been climbed using aid by the Spaniards as a variation to Original Route and rejoined that route on the small ledges. Unfortunately, it was dripping with water and looked choked with moss and lichen.

They chose the Spanish variation and hoped it would dry with fine weather. Barry led the first part and commented afterwards: 'I was really surprised at how wet and slimy it was. Dry, it would be really good climbing with lots of little features. But every time I tried to jam my hands in, it was just like putting them in mud and gave me no confidence.'

It was obvious that in order to free-climb the crack they would have to clean it to reveal hidden holds for their fingers and rock shoes. This process was possible only by first using aid from pegs, nuts and friends to climb the crack, then, on reaching the ledges, abseiling back down, scraping the moss from the crack and scrubbing dirt and lichen away with a wire brush. The long, tiring industrial-like procedure would take them three days of hard work to complete, but it was necessary if they were to have any chance of free-climbing the route.

They progressed without incident until the following day, when Nancy was confronted by a very difficult section of aid climbing. After she had made slow progress by placing and pulling up on poor and insecure friends and nuts, the crack became flared, wide on the outside and rapidly narrowing to a hairline crack in the back. Friends and nuts would not lodge well enough to support her weight, and she could hardly place pegs in the back as the crack constricted the swing of her hammer. The Spaniards had given this section the difficult artificial grade of A3; Nancy, who was more used to free-climbing, thought it was harder. Eventually, she managed to hammer in a peg a quarter of an inch (6 mm) into which she clipped her two etriers. She stood in the etriers and held her breath, fearful that the peg would pull. She then stepped higher in the etriers to reach further up the crack. The peg still held. Then at full stretch she managed to jam a cam into the back of the crack. Happier at finding this placement, she clipped her etriers into it and stepped up. With her face now level with the cam, she could see that it was only wedged behind a small crystal and could pop out at any time. Heart pounding and frantic to find a more secure placement, she tried to place another peg. It was too late. With a loud pop the cam pulled out and she fell backwards. The force of the fall ripped out the peg below and now, as her body gained momentum, it ripped out the nuts and friends below like a giant zip undoing.

A dramatic illustration showing only a small part of the face taken from the peak opposite. The climbers are just visible on the third pitch of the Spanish variation and are about to reach the small ledge where they erected the Portaledge.

'Catch me! *Pull in the rope!*' Nancy had time to cry urgently.

The fall went on for ever. All Barry can remember was the noise. A piercing scream followed by a metallic crash and a blonde explosion of hair flying earthwards as Nancy's body, with all the climbing hardware, hit the wall above Barry. He gripped the rope tight and waited for the pull. It took a long time coming, but eventually the rope stretched as one of the pieces of protection held and she came to an ungainly stop hanging in mid-air. From Barry's viewpoint the 40-foot (12-m) fall looked and sounded bad.

'You all right Nancy?' Barry shouted urgently.

At first there was no response and he tried again: 'Nancy?'

'Phew! Yeah that was a bit longer fall than I expected,' Nancy croaked. Then in a worried voice she said: 'I've bruised my foot pretty bad and my hand's hurting.'

Nancy was fortunate that, despite hitting the wall, her injuries were superficial, and with new determination she climbed back up the rope to battle with the crack again, apprehensive at repeating the whole process but feeling confident that she could work out a better way of placing the gear. It was still touch and go but eventually, and with great relief, she made the hanging bolt belay stance that the Spaniards had placed. Although Nancy could be described as physically petite she had phenomenal mental drive and simply never gave up. Barry described her as 'having a prize fighter's heart'.

On the third day of working the crack it rained, but they still persevered, first climbing the ropes to their high point. In fact, Barry was in his element aiding up the top part of the crack. 'I felt like my hero, Walter Bonatti, up there in the rain and in my big mountain boots. Like a real alpinist. My kind of climbing!'

At the end of the day Nancy knew she had the ability to climb it free – but did she have the time to prove it? The weather had been reasonable and the crack had dried considerably; even the waterfall was now only a trickle. With only three days left, a careful plan of action was crucial. She suggested it would take her two more days to free the crack, then they could bivouac on the ledges for the night and go for the top in a really long day. Although the ledges were only half-way up the face, the upper half of the climb, according to the Spaniards' information, was much easier than the lower section.

A free ascent was becoming really important to Nancy. She said:

I enjoy free-climbing so much and that's where my challenge is. It's not an adventure for some people, but it is for me. Barry and I are compatible. His strong points are his incredible endurance and his support and the way he rallied me when I was tired. It meant a lot to me when Barry hauled all the gear up the face one day, letting me conserve energy for my free-climbing attempts.

But Barry knew that he did not have the ability to free-climb the crack, and on one occasion announced impatiently: 'I want to get up it any way I can.'

It was the voice of a mountaineer who saw conquering the mountain as more important than wasting all this time on a free ascent, time that could be spent getting to the top by pulling on a few pegs and nuts. He was also very concerned that they could easily fail due to lack of time. Under the pressure of the situation their different backgrounds and aspirations were coming to the fore.

Barry, laughing, praised Nancy: 'It was like the rapier and the mace – myself being the mace. It was great to have Nancy lead the route, putting the rope above me like a rock gun. She's a brilliant granite climber, beautiful and inspirational to watch. I soon fell into the role of beast of burden, hauling bags and aid climbing in the rain!'

The free attempt on the crack started the following day with Barry having the first try. The early summer mountaineering on the snow slopes of Peru had not been the ideal training for gymnastic rock-climbing and he soon had to rest by hanging on nuts. 'I was not willing to fall. It's an old alpinist habit I've got, and I will use anything to avoid falling in the mountains. So when I started thrashing and trembling I used some aluminium laybacks and a nylon foothold – as long as there was a piece of gear to grab I was OK.'

Barry's attempt at free-climbing over, he gained the first stance as quickly as he could by pulling on more nuts. Nancy then followed and gracefully climbed the pitch free, grading it hard 5.10.

The next pitch was much harder, and, finding the crack rounded and holdless, Nancy face-climbed on either side of the crack using little flakes and black knobs of harder rock typical of the region. She was in her element and soon completed the pitch, which she thought rated hard 5.11. Above the stance the rock looked

steep, and the crack narrowed then doglegged around an overhang. It looked the crux of the climb, and Nancy suggested descending then returning to try it the following day when she would be fresh for the difficult climbing. They would also collect their bivouac gear so that they could stay the night on the ledges and attempt to complete the climb the day after.

Back on the route, Nancy battled hard with the pitch, working out each sequence of moves, but there was a 30-foot (9-m) section without any gear to protect a fall. Lacking this protection, she was reluctant to try to lead the crux pitch free. A bolt or two would have solved the problem, but unfortunately the drill had been left at base camp. Really disappointed at failing to lead the pitch free but resigned to the fact that time had now run out, Nancy climbed their fixed rope up to the ledges. As a consolation Barry lowered her back down the pitch, which she then free-climbed on a top-rope (protected by a rope from above), grading it 5.12.

Both the American first ascensionists and the Spaniards had used the ledges to sleep on before climbing to the top. With modern equipment this was not as uncomfortable or dangerous as the image of being perched on a narrow 1-foot ledge 1000 feet (305 m) up a vertical face suggests. A special hammock, called a Portaledge, is fixed to the wall; when draped and tensioned correctly with tubular aluminium poles, the hammock forms a rectangular nylon ledge 6 feet by 4 feet (1.8 m by 1.2 m) – big enough for two people to lie down and sleep. A nylon fly-sheet drapes over the Portaledge to protect the occupants from the elements.

Barry had never slept in one before, 'Though I remember plenty of times in the past when I should have had one but didn't!'

He took the lead in trying to construct the structure while Nancy offered suggestions. Unfortunately, what the manufacturers describe as 'a simple job to erect' turned into a farce: 'I think you have it inside out' and 'Try putting the pole in the other way around' were typical suggestions. It was a frustrating job made worse by ensuring that nothing was dropped while they hung in space

Erecting the Portaledge half-way up the face. This hanging tent is suspended on two bolt anchors and has an aluminium frame which supports a sleeping platform just big enough for two.

with a bundle of nylon and metal tubes which seemed to have a life of their own. Eventually, a combined effort overpowered the nylon and they had their home for the night hanging from a couple of bolts just above the ledge. They unpacked their sleeping-bags, food, water and stove from the 'haulbag', which they had hauled up to the ledges, and settled down for the evening. They used a specially designed cylinder-gas stove which they could hang on the rock just outside the fly-sheet. They took turns at cooking soup, dehydrated meals with spaghetti, beef jerky, biscuits and candy bars washed down with tea and instant cappuccino. Dinner with a view!

They were just settling down in their sleeping-bags and adjusting their safety rope, to which they were still attached, when the inevitable happened.

'Oh, no,' Barry said to himself, knowing the disturbance and rigmarole that going to the lavatory would cause. Up until recently it was normal practice to drop your pants (harnesses are designed so you can do this while still staying securely tied to the rope) and doing whatever you wanted to do into space. While this is still acceptable practice when you urinate, defecating is a different matter as more people climb and environmental good practice is aspired to by the majority (in fact, faeces are classed as biomedical waste in Canada). Barry followed the recommended procedure and took a good aim into a strong plastic bag which he then stored with the cooking rubbish to be taken off the climb.

An early start was essential if they were going to complete the climb that day, so after an oatmeal and coffee breakfast they had the Portaledge and gear packed away by five and were climbing soon after. Two relatively easy pitches of 5.9 climbing up the corner system above took them to an obvious 150-foot (46-m) traverse line which was also straightforward but featured a number of unpleasantly loose blocks. At the end of the traverse, a corner system led all the way to the summit ridge 500 feet (152 m) above. The granite of the upper half of the climb was more weathered, and Barry was again in his element as the route took on a more classical alpine character. It was only 8 a.m. and, full of confidence at quickly reaching the summit, they continued. Easier than expected, they thought. How wrong they were!

Although they found the weather a bit hot and clammy, they could not have predicted the huge cumulo-nimbus cloud building up out of sight on the other side of the mountain and steadily approaching. Two pitches higher, and the clouds appeared over the summit ridge like a giant grey-black ghoul. At first they did not notice it, so engrossed were they in the climbing, but a sudden gust of wind and the rock thrown into shadow by the spectre soon brought the dramatic change of weather to their attention.

The thunder started as a growl which they felt in their stomachs and reached a crescendo-like drum-roll. It got darker, then there was a flash, and a whipcrack went up their spines as a shaft of lightning hit the peak opposite. Hail the size of bullets pelted them, and the deluge was so intense that it was impossible to look up. In a minute everything was white.

Perversely, Barry thought, Ah good. I'm an alpinist, I can deal with this! I've seen this before.

Most climbers are terrified of lightning, often more so than avalanches or stonefalls – an understandable fear, as rock peaks like Proboscis are no more than giant lightning conductors. Barry recalled later:

> We were totally committed only 200 feet (61 m) below the summit. It was terrifying. A primeval fear hot-wired to your brain. The way I deal with it is to intellectually work out the safest options. Too high to abandon the climb and descend, yet suicidal to continue. We just had to hope the storm would pass and sit it out.

An hour of hell passed very slowly, but just as suddenly as the storm arrived it disappeared and blue sky reappeared above. There was now a sense of urgency as the conditions for lightning build-up were ideal, and they could hear the distant rumble of more storms that could hit them at any time. Unfortunately, the rock was completely soaked by the melted hail, and climbing on slippery lichen-covered rock above was going to be a real test. Barry's drive and experience as a mountaineer now came to the fore in this adverse situation, and he coolly climbed the rock above to within a stone's throw of the summit ridge. Nancy took over the lead

Barry reaching the summit ridge as a storm cloud boils all round. He described it as like a cathedral roof covered in lichen as slippery as snakes' snot.

but could not find the correct line; frustratingly, each time she thought she'd cracked it she was led up a blind alley. She could see the summit ridge but the rock above her was holdless. Disturbingly, the wind had picked up again and clouds started to boil overhead. Their epic was continuing and another storm was about to hit them.

TRAVELLING TO THE CIRQUE

At the present time there is no easy, or for that matter inexpensive, way to travel to the Cirque. Moreover, the weather can often be unpredictable, and in order for aircraft and helicopters to operate in the most efficient manner over large distances climbing parties may need to fit into a schedule that includes commercial operations such as mining and other leisure pursuits like river rafting. During periods of bad weather flights can stack up so a flexible timetable is essential, but the charter operators we used were efficient, highly experienced and keen to offer value for money.

Scheduled airline services operate to both Whitehorse in the Yukon and to Fort Simpson in Northwest Territories. From either town it is possible to hire fixed-wing aircraft and helicopters, and while it has been traditional for climbers to fly in from Whitehorse the facilities available at Fort Simpson may well be more useful. South Nahanni Airways (Jacques Harvey, pilot, Laverna Martel, office manager, tel: 001 403 695 2007/3114; fax: 001 403 695 2943) fly from Fort Simpson to Glacier Lake, and Great Slave Helicopters (Jim Broadbent, base manager and pilot, tel: 001 403 695 2326; fax: 001 403 873 6087) will provide uplift to the Cirque itself. Both Jacques and Jim are hugely experienced bush operators and aware of climbers' needs.

Obviously, economies can be made if a team occupies the whole of a plane and partially laden trips are avoided. The Tourist Officer in Fort Simpson, Clarence Villeneuve (tel: 001 403 695 7230; fax 001 403 695 2381), is incredibly helpful: born and raised in this small community, he is a natural ambassador for all its peoples. He is a fund of information, offers a level of service that is hard to beat, and is happy to advise climbers on all aspects of their trip. Like all small communities, Fort Simpson operates in a way that is not always obvious to outsiders, but if Clarence says that something can be fixed, it can!

With a cry of relief she found a hidden hold and pulled on to easier ground just as her rope jammed in a crack. Nothing was going right. She belayed and Barry climbed up to free the offending rope. Quickly he reached Nancy and, concentrating on climbing fast, passed her without a word and reached the summit ridge.

Oh man, what a surprise when I reached the ridge. It was like the edge of a cathedral roof, with lichen as slippery as snakes' snot on the north side and vertical granite on the other side. I looked at the boiling clouds and then at the summit 150 feet (46 m) over on the right. It would have been foolhardy to linger, and we had to descend straight away down the south ridge to the left. I would have loved to have gone to the summit. It's not the whole mountain, but it's a more important piece than most. Classically, it is why the whole endeavour began.

The second storm hit the mountain as Barry reached the belay on the ridge, but luck was with them and the main body of clouds passed to the north.

Nancy recalls: 'I wanted to turn off my brain but couldn't. I was soaked, cold and tired, but we had to keep mentally aware until we reached safety.'

After a fortnight of effort they had reached their goal. But for the storm they could have gone to the summit, relaxed and enjoyed the view. Instead they had to hurry down.

Airlie Anderson and Aid Burgess

Utah Roadtrip, USA

4

The temperature dropped and it started snowing as Aid and Airlie walked up the canyon. They ignored the deteriorating weather at first but later, as they hung off the belay in the middle of the huge vertical expanse of ice, flakes the size of golf balls filled the sky. It was the type of snow that gives Utah 'the greatest skiing on earth' but it was turning their situation into a nightmare. The build-up of snow in the basin above, whipped up by strong gusts of wind, released wave after wave of spindrift avalanches that swept the ice, and Aid was extremely anxious about setting out on the committing second pitch.

With a worried voice he said: 'I'll give it a go, but if it gets much worse we'll have to get out of here. Watch that rope carefully: it's really steep and the ice is rotten as hell!'

Aid moved slowly across the brittle ice, formed like a chandelier by the constant dripping of freezing water, his ice tools barely holding. Frustratingly, each time he tried to place protection the ice shattered or was hollow and full of air holes.

Aid Burgess leads the difficult top pitch of Back Off in Santaquin Canyon. He has overcome the steepest part, which is just above Airlie Anderson who is belayed on the side of the ice below.

UTAH'S DESERT CLIMBING HISTORY

With the exception of unrecorded ascents by local Indians, the first big tower to be climbed was by John Otto in 1911 when he climbed the 500-foot (152-m) Independence Monument in Colorado National Monument (on the border between Utah and Colorado). He climbed it by artificial means, chipping large holds and drilling holes to insert metal rods. The rods have been removed, but his route still uses the manufactured holds and is graded II 5.8+.

The next notable desert-climb was made in 1939, when Brower, Robinson, Bedayn and Dyer climbed Shiprock, just over the border in New Mexico, graded III 5.7 A2 (now 5.9 free). But even then the desert canyonlands remained virtually uncharted, and it was not until the early 1950s that climbers became aware of the potential. Then, in 1956, Yosemite-trained climbers scaled the fabulous 800-foot (244-m) Spider Rock. The decade that followed is regarded as the golden age of desert-climbing, when climbers from California and Colorado began ascending such dramatic pinnacles as The Totem Pole and Standing Rock, Castleton Tower and The Titan. In particular, Layton Kor, Huntley Ingalls, Fred Beckey and Harvey Carter were instrumental in establishing many significant ascents. When in 1962 climbers came into conflict with the Navahos, climbing was banned on Spider Rock and Totem Pole, which have particular religious significance for the Indians.

Moses Tower was climbed for the first time by the North Face Route (Pale Fire V 5.8 A3, now free at 5.12) in 1972 by Beckey, Bjørnstad, Galvin, Nephew and Markov.

The second wave of development started in the late 1970s and was helped particularly by the invention of the Friend by Ray Jardine in 1979. This device allowed the parallel sandstone cracks to be protected much more easily and with greater security, resulting in an explosion of free climbing throughout the desert. Areas such as Indian Creek were developed for free-climbing (starting with the ascent of Super Crack in 1976) and many towers were free-climbed. Numerous talented climbers were involved in the development, but Ed Webster, Erlc Bjørnstad and Rob Slater were particularly influential.

Zion National Park has a separate climbing history starting in the 1920s, with many artificial big wall-climbs being developed until the late 1970s. Since then the emphasis has been on making hammerless ascents or free ascents of these or new routes. This is typified by Peter Croft and Johnny Woodward when they free-climbed Moolight Buttress in 1992 to establish probably the hardest sandstone route in the world at V 5.13b.

'Watch it. Hell! This is impossible. I can't see my feet. The snow's covering everything.'

Airlie shivered with apprehension and cold. Although she was dressed for the weather and the belay was in a slight scoop, partially protecting her from above, the snow still continually deluged her. She could think of better places to be right now!

With rare fear in his voice, Aid shouted through the howling wind: 'I'm coming back – if I can! The spindrift is knocking me off. Watch the rope!'

So ended Aid's and Airlie's first day climbing together.

I t is hard to find two climbers with more diverse backgrounds than Aid Burgess and Airlie Anderson. Separated in age by over 25 years, they come from two very different climbing traditions, but despite this each had expressed a desire to partner the other and so the idea of a climbing trip in the States was born. Airlie had limited experience of travelling, having flown only once before (on a shuttle trip to Scotland), and her foreign travel was limited to the French Alps. Aid, on the other hand, was a seasoned world traveller but with atti-

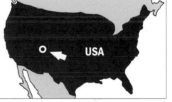

tudes still moulded in the 1970s rather than those of the new generation of rock-climbers that Airlie represented. For both the next week would be a new experience.

Airlie Anderson is a stocky figure of about 5 feet 4 inches (1.6 m) tall who normally dresses in black. Her dark blonde hair is tightly plaited and she constantly wears a cap even when climbing. Street-wise and cool, she will only rarely admit to being impressed and certainly was not going to be intimidated by Aid's experience and reputation. Brought up in Essex, she speaks with a pronounced accent and, with a habit of articulating her first thoughts immediately, she is usually forthright and blunt. Among some climbers she has a reputation for being opinionated, moody and unreliable, but this probably has as much to do with insecurity as with arrogance. Moreover, her unconventional approach to the sport (typified by her tackling some of climbing's most demanding test pieces early in her career) has upset many of the male traditionalists who have doubtless been threatened by her precocious ability.

Airlie was born in 1974; her parents are separated and she is distanced from her father. She knows her mother better but says she did not get on with her. Airlie's secondary education was at an all-female comprehensive from which she was eventually expelled over an incident regarded as bullying (although Airlie pointedly claims that the other girl was bigger than her) but not before she had discovered an interest in climbing. This had developed when she had her first encounter with an indoor climbing wall during a school trip. On realizing she was better than her class-mates, she instantly took a liking to the sport and, bitten by the climbing bug, started going to a local wall three times a week. Within a couple of months, climbing had become the centrepiece of her life, providing a new horizon but alienating Airlie from her friends. At the age of 16, and with a boyfriend she had met while climbing, Airlie moved north to the city that is traditionally regarded (especially by those who live there) as the centre of English climbing – Sheffield. 'My life began on the way to Sheffield,' she says of that journey, adding that she thought the streets themselves would be paved with chalk!

Aid and Airlie gearing up below Moses Tower. Aid is carrying a large rack of gear necessary to protect long sandstone climbs.

Too young to claim the dole, she lived on £25 a month and found plenty of time in which to develop her talent on rock. She was one of the first women to attempt many of the hardest routes, including an early repeat of Master's Edge (E7, 6b) at Millstone, which she found physically very hard. She was finally successful here, using pre-placed protection and a mattress at the bottom in case she fell. Her success was motivated by a simple need: 'I wanted to prove that I wasn't a complete wimp.' Beginner's Mind (E7/8, 6c) on the Dinas Mot boulders in Llanberis Pass was another success. Here she made the fifth ascent, although she tried the route only because others were attempting it and she was not going to be left out.

Among traditionalists, Airlie's climbing has often proved as controversial as her fiery personality. On Beginner's Mind, for example, her ascent was achieved over a period of two days during which she top-roped then yo-yoed the route, a practice used by previous ascenders of the route. Criticized by what she called 'the sad bunch of Sheffield armchair critics', she punched one of them in a pub following an argument over her methods, and retorted by stating in an interview:

> Men have been using these tactics, and much worse, to do hard trad. routes since the beginning of time without anyone batting an eyelid. As soon as a woman does, everyone suddenly jumps on their high horses about it. There are too many male egos on the climbing scene, who find it hard to come to terms with the amount of women equalling or bettering their climbing achievements, and find the only way to deal with it is to put them down and find fault with whatever they do.

In fact her achievement was, at the time, the hardest traditional lead by a British woman, but unlike the majority of climbers Airlie had no sense of the sport's rich history. Also, lacking any semblance of modesty, she simply appeared to be picking off a series of hard routes that were climbed in any style necessary to get her to the top. More recently, Airlie admits she has had a change of focus from seeing climbing as the *only* thing that mattered in her life to it becoming part of a broader picture. 'If you are only climbing,' Airlie reasons, 'it can be quite negative. It meant that if I had a bad day climbing, everything was bad.'

The gritstone moors in the Peak District National Park outside Sheffield's city boundaries still provide her favourite routes, but she has also become attracted to the mountains of North Wales and the limestone cliffs of Pembrokeshire in the far south-west of the country. Yet if Airlie's achievements are entirely on rock, it is in the world's high ranges that Adrian Burgess is most at home.

In physical terms Aid contrasts sharply with Airlie. A lanky, strong figure, his 6-foot (1.8 m) frame is crowned by a distinctive mop of blond hair. He usually dresses casually in a comfortable style that has not changed much with the passing years, and he lets garments hang from him rather than wear them, giving an impression that his interests lie elsewhere. Aid and his brother Alan are identical twins. For many years it was virtually impossible to tell them apart, and they used this physical similarity to confuse strangers – not least members of the opposite sex. Today it is easier to tell which twin is which ('Al's a vegetarian, so he's just

A SHORT GUIDE TO UTAH ICE-CLIMBING

The Wasatch Range of mountains in Utah is one of the most important areas for ice-climbing in the States. All the routes are of the water ice/ice-fall variety and are in their best condition from late November through to early March. Grades, where known, are given in parentheses.

Provo Canyon is the most popular area, with the 1000-foot (305-m) Stairway to Heaven (W5) being the plum. Other worthwhile routes are Bridal Veil Right Side, Finger of Fate, Miller's Thriller and The Fang. Half a dozen other routes exist but in most years the ice does not form thickly enough. Post Nasal Drip is probably the hardest of the bunch.

Santaquin Canyon contains five great climbs, though Candlestick, Squashhead (W4) and Back Off (W5) are the only three that consistently form. Although only 200 feet (61 m) long, they are of excellent quality. Angel of Fear (W6+) and Automatic Control Theory are two of the harder ice-fall routes in the States but often do not form.

Little Cottonwood Canyon, on the outskirts of Salt Lake City, has two excellent intermediate-grade climbs, The Great White Icicle and Scruffy Band.

Other ice-climbs can be found in Big Cottonwood Canyon, American Fork Canyon, Maple Canyon, Ogden Canyon, Waterfall Canyon, Sundance and North Creek Canyon.

withering away,' is Aid's scientific explanation of this), but they are still tied by an incredibly close bond that goes back to their earliest years. To outsiders they seem an indomitable duo who have spent their lives on a long roller-coaster ride careering recklessly from one improbable exploit to another.

'The twins', as they are universally known within climbing circles, are at the heart of a strong anarchic streak in British mountaineering which rebels at any notion of conformity or acceptance of officialdom. Their jointly written *The Burgess Book of Lies* has added to this myth, with its tales of mayhem and confusion through three decades and across four continents.

They began climbing while still schoolboys at Holmfirth in West Yorkshire and immediately found life outside the classroom preferable to that inside. Since then, Aid has climbed around the globe. Notable ascents, many of which have been undertaken in the company of Alan, include an early ascent of the Central Pillar of Frêney in the French Alps, the Cassin Spur of Mount McKinley in Alaska, Fitzroy and Cerro Torre in Patagonia, and Dhaulagiri, Annapurna IV and Everest in the Himalayas. These achievements are all the greater when you consider that the twins are survivors from a highly ambitious generation of British climbers, many of whom have died, paying the ultimate price for their success.

Since the early 1980s Aid has adopted a more conventional existence and is now married to Lorna, whom he first met in Nepal. She is one of America's top immigration lawyers and they live outside Salt Lake City in Utah where, coincidentally, Alan is now based. Friends who have known Aid over the years look at his present lifestyle with wry amusement, for when not on one of his frequent expeditions, Aid minds the house, brews copious quantities of fine but extremely potent beer and shares his partner's love of horse-riding. The Aid Burgess of the 1990s is no longer extricating himself from innumerable scrapes involving women, alcohol, a sense of natural justice, or all three, but hunting with Utah's smart set.

Yet there are still flashes of the old Aid left, so it seemed safer for Airlie to travel to the States than for Aid to come to Britain. Teaming up two people with such strong personalities could make for an explosive combination. Separated by age, outlook and interests, there could be as much forcing them apart as bringing them together.

Before leaving England Airlie had started to read *The Burgess Book of Lies* but had stopped, saying emphatically, 'I don't want to be overawed by him', while Aid, making no concessions to political correctness, said with his characteristic wicked grin, 'This sounds like a hell of a chick'.

Originally they had envisaged a road trip that would also take in Red Rocks outside Las Vegas, but a shortage of time had focused their minds on two objectives: a demanding ice-climb at Santaquin, some 70 miles (113 km) due south of Salt Lake City, to be followed, later in the week, by a long drive south-east to Moab to tackle Primrose Dihedrals on Moses Tower, which is often acclaimed as the finest desert climb in North America.

Desert towers seemed a long way off, however, as Aid and Airlie returned to their down-at-heel motel after their miserable first day of ice-climbing was prematurely halted by a storm. Snow was still falling, and a despondent air was fuelled by the local television station's weather presenter standing on what he described as 'our weather porch' warning about another big storm blowing in from the west. The broadcasts would be starting early on the following morning, 'so you'll know if it's possible to make it in to the office'. For Aid's and Airlie's particular line of work, the forecast was distinctly unhopeful.

Next morning, as they peered out of the steamed motel window into a cold, grey early light, they realized that the warning had been over-enthusiastic. In fact the storm had been less serious than predicted and had blown itself out during the night. Breakfast was a visit to D'Arcey's Diner with the usual temptations to over-eat, before heading out on Interstate 15.

They dodged the monstrous, chrome-gleaming articulated trucks that were out in convoy heading for Vegas or beyond, and at the Santaquin intersection Aid pulled off the Interstate and headed up the narrow snow-covered road that gave access to the Santaquin Canyon, where some of Utah's hardest ice-climbs are found. With snowflakes still in the air and the previous day fresh in their minds, Aid and Airlie decided to walk up just for a look and to attempt the climb again only if the weather improved.

Airlie leading the first pitch of Back Off. By swinging the pick of her ice tools into the ice and then kicking in her crampon points, even the steepest ice can be climbed.

The walk up the canyon was beautiful. The storm had laid down a deep and uniform blanket of powder snow, and the branches of the conifer trees buckled under the weight. The stillness was broken only by Aid's and Airlie's intermittent chatter.

'Do you ice-climb because you want to become a mountaineer?' asked Aid. Airlie rarely used sentences or paused to take a breath, and her answer was delivered in her typical quick-fire way:

> I'd love to be able to go into mountains and perhaps one day go to the Himalayas, but I don't know whether I'll be able to because maybe I just won't enjoy it and maybe I'll be too scared or maybe I'll be crap at altitude or never have the money or never get round to it. In the long term, though, I see my climbing developing in those terms, but I do like ice-climbing just as an end in itself.

Aid countered with:

> My brother and I had a classic apprenticeship starting on rock, then ice, in Scotland. After that the Alps and then the Himalayas, but I think people now specialize more. A lot more sport climbers in the States are starting ice-climbing, especially on the accessible ice-falls near the road. It's kind of fashionable with the 'weekend warrior'! But I don't think it would be as popular over here if you had to walk a couple of hours and the weather was always bad, like Scotland.

Airlie added:

> It's become fashionable in Britain as well, but whether people are enjoying it or just enjoying the idea of doing it I'm not sure. I enjoy it, but it would only take a couple of bad experiences and I could see myself turning off ice. I've only had one trip to Scotland, one to Wales and a week in Chamonix. To improve I need to climb lots more ice, practise leading easier stuff and second-ing harder climbs, especially to realize what I can do to test myself, experiment and learn, but mainly lots more leading climbs because that's what I enjoy.

Further up, the limestone cliffs increased in height and the canyon narrowed. Through gaps in the trees, tantalizing glimpses of 200-foot (61-m) waterfalls of ice could be seen cascading down the cliffs, frozen in time like giant melted wax candles. It was obvious why this area had a reputation for some of the best and most difficult ice-climbs in the States, with the narrow gorge protecting the ice from the sun between November and March. Aid pointed out Angel of Fear and Automatic Control Theory, desperate examples of overhanging ice-climbing on slender pencils of free-standing ice which rarely form thickly enough to climb. This year was no exception, and Aid and Airlie continued walking through the snow to their intended climb called Back Off, an apt description considering their retreat from it the day before.

Back Off was one of the first routes in Santaquin to be climbed (in 1978) and it still has a reputation as a classic hard ice-climb, being graded W5 (standing for a Waterfall Ice grade 5 in a system where 1 is easy and 7 is desperate). The main feature is a 150-foot-high (46-m-high) sheet of ice usually only a foot thick cascading over a sheer limestone wall.

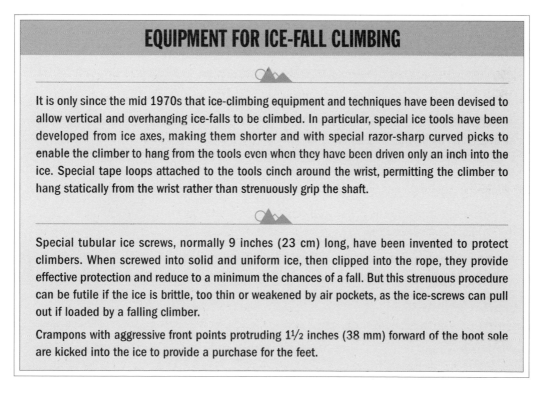

EQUIPMENT FOR ICE-FALL CLIMBING

It is only since the mid 1970s that ice-climbing equipment and techniques have been devised to allow vertical and overhanging ice-falls to be climbed. In particular, special ice tools have been developed from ice axes, making them shorter and with special razor-sharp curved picks to enable the climber to hang from the tools even when they have been driven only an inch into the ice. Special tape loops attached to the tools cinch around the wrist, permitting the climber to hang statically from the wrist rather than strenuously grip the shaft.

Special tubular ice screws, normally 9 inches (23 cm) long, have been invented to protect climbers. When screwed into solid and uniform ice, then clipped into the rope, they provide effective protection and reduce to a minimum the chances of a fall. But this strenuous procedure can be futile if the ice is brittle, too thin or weakened by air pockets, as the ice-screws can pull out if loaded by a falling climber.

Crampons with aggressive front points protruding 1½ inches (38 mm) forward of the boot sole are kicked into the ice to provide a purchase for the feet.

The new snow made the approach heavy going, particularly the steep slope from the canyon base to the bottom of the climb, but Aid's powerful 6-foot (1.8-m) frame, honed to fitness from years of serious training and work as a 'snow-plough' battling his way up Himalayan giants, made light work of it, while Airlie was happy following Aid's footsteps, being more used to the drive and short walks to gritstone crags around Sheffield than the grind and hard labour of mountaineering. After an hour they reached the base of the climb and stopped at the ledge they had cut in the hard old snow the day before. Though bitterly cold, the weather had improved and the spindrift avalanches had stopped, so they geared up, hoping for more success than they'd had on their previous attempt.

Airlie quickly led the straightforward first section of the climb. This initial 'pitch' was up easy snow-covered ice, and she only stopped twice to place ice-screw protection where the climb steepened. Soon she was hanging securely from the belay.

In a revealing insight into her strong views on climbing motivation she said:

I found the pitch quite easy but psychologically I needed to lead it to feel that I contributed to the climb. If all you do is second, then you get a sec-onder's head, where you feel second best, you are the one that is not as good and you have to sit on the belay and wait, watch and wonder what is happening for ages while the leader has all the fun. They are the one that gets to sit on the top and have the nice view and feel good, then all you do is struggle for ages getting their ice-screws out! In general I don't think that seconding is as enjoyable. There is a big difference, though, between leading and seconding in the danger aspect, and at the moment I haven't had enough experience on ice to think of leading the hard top pitch.

Aid speedily joined her and carefully racked his gear for the difficult pitch above.

Ice-climbing is all about strength, technique and confidence – but mainly con-fidence. It is a mind game that is usually a lot more serious than rock-climbing. In short, your mind says, No way am I going up there, it's ridiculous, but you have to persuade yourself that you can do it. Unfortunately Aid's confidence had taken a mighty battering on the previous attempt and he set off very tentatively. Carefully and slowly he traversed across the brittle ice, and by the time he reached better conditions his arms were exhausted. As he admitted:

> The main problem was that the new snow covered all the bumps and ripples in the ice which indicate the best placements. Normally I would immediately see the best place to plant my tools and where to stand with my crampons, but because of the conditions I spent a long time scratching around and clearing snow – and even then I was often not happy with my placements. Once doubt came into my mind I started to question the holding power of the tools in the ice. I placed them again and again to make sure and then found myself gripping the shaft too tight. I was wasting time, and my arms were draining of strength.

Aid hung precariously, trying to rest, but with hands above his head holding his ice tools and his calves screaming as he strained to stand on the front points of his crampons, he could not regain any strength.

Relax. Relax. Hold it together. Keep moving, he tried to convince himself as he managed to place a good ice-screw in the better ice at the end of the traverse. At least he had protection against a fall. Above was the steepest part of the climb consisting of a 20-foot (6-m) section of vertical, smooth ice. Normally Aid would have revelled in the challenge and romped up the ice with strength to spare, but all athletes have their off days and today he was struggling. He knew the best ploy would be to climb the steep section without stopping, then to rest and place ice-screw protection where the angle eased above. Unfortunately, after he had climbed 10 feet (3 m) the last protection looked a long, long way below, and he stopped at the steepest point to place another screw – he was playing it safe, but the process tired him even more. With his strength running out, Aid began to question his capacity to finish the route.

But Aid's phenomenal record as a world-class mountaineer had not been gained by giving up whenever the going got tough; it was one of those times when you have to dig deep into both physical and mental reserves.

'I looked up and the ice seemed to go on for ever – on and on. From then it was a stamina problem; of not fading in terms of power and of trying to conserve strength.'

With the steepest part behind him, Aid carefully moved up. Placing one ice tool, testing it for holding power, then placing the second tool and testing it, then moving his feet up by swinging his foot and kicking the crampon points into the ice… slowly his confidence grew and with it his strength.

'It's amazing that when you start moving fluidly you climb quickly, and I was 15 feet (4½ m) higher before I knew it.' A couple more stops to place ice-screw protection and success was in sight as he tackled the final bulge of ice before the top.

'I'm safe. Taking in the rope,' Aid croaked, his throat still dry from his efforts.

'That's me – climbing,' Airlie's voice drifted up from below.

'OK.'

Airlie took hold of her new Predator ice tools. Instruments described by the blacksmith of horror-writing, Stephen King, as the most violent-looking articles created by man. (He wrote: 'I want to drive the pick end into wood – to envision how easily this same tip could penetrate the skull and skewer the soft grey matter beneath… You could do some big damage with this. Real big damage. I want one for Christmas – not for climbing, but to keep under my bed!') Airlie's thoughts were of climbing, not violence, but because she had been hanging on the belay for over an hour, the inactivity had frozen her to the bone. In particular she could not feel her fingers, and this made gripping her Predators much harder. She was also very apprehensive, having seen Aid struggle, especially with all his years of experience. As she moved tentatively across the first traverse her hands started to warm, but as the feeling slowly came back so did the sickening pain of 'hot aches' as the blood began to pump through her fingers.

'Oh, oh! This is desperate!' Airlie groaned. Hanging from one axe and then the other, shaking her hands alternately, trying to warm them up, she almost cried with pain. Eventually, warmth came back to her fingers and she started climbing again. With the rope protecting her from above and benefiting from her rock-climbing strength, she swung her Predators confidently, they entered the ice with a dull *thwack* and she trusted the placements first time. Even though she was a relative novice at this winter game, she powered up the steep section and soon began to enjoy the climbing above. With calves straining from standing on her crampon points and arms tired from the brutal steepness, she pulled over the final bulge of ice and with a big, happy smile reached Aid at the top.

Pressurized by time and weather, Airlie's only impressions of this predominantly Mormon community were gained in odd moments. Finding restaurants reluctant to serve beer or just sensing that she did not fit in to a community that puts a high price on family values and hard work were as much insight as a hectic schedule allowed. Frantic packing of a Ford Explorer, which was not as cavernous as it looked, followed the ice-climb. Aid and Airlie were clearing their motel rooms in late afternoon stuffing personal and climbing gear into every part of the four by four. There was a full desert climbing-rack, tents, stoves and clothing – and also a set of 'growlers', large glass containers, of which there were seven or eight to be filled with beer from a micro-brewery in Moab where Aid conveniently knew the owner. Despite a shortage of space, Aid insisted that these jars were an essential part of the gear. 'Look, Airlie,' he reasoned, 'we're going to the desert and there ain't no beer there… I mean, there ain't no water there either, but there certainly ain't no beer.'

Finally, in the way of America's drive-and-go culture, Airlie got a coffee and some food from the gas station and Aid an eight-pack, and the drive south began. To an outsider Utah appears to be one of the most repressive states, with tough alcohol and speeding laws, but none of this seemed to matter on this particular evening. Daylight faded rapidly, the radio got tuned to a country station, Airlie put on headphones for a private dose of hard-core techno music and the miles started to drift by. Places with improbable names and indeterminable history slid by in the darkness. Scipio, Salina, Freemont Junction and Green River came and went until, mid-evening and 200 miles (322 km) later, there was a final right turn at Crescent Junction, a winding descent alongside the railroad track and then into Moab itself. They arrived just after 9 p.m. and Airlie and Aid found that the journey had taken them not just from one climate to another but also to a different culture. This is a laid-back town, the outdoor adventure capital of the desert, where climbers mix with mountain bikers and white-water rafters.

Moses Tower is in Canyonlands National Park where, unlike in Britain, permits are needed to camp in the park itself. For a visitor from abroad the situation can

It took over two hours to drive into Taylor Canyon in the heart of the Canyonlands National Park. Moses Tower can be seen on the left, separated from the main sandstone escarpment.

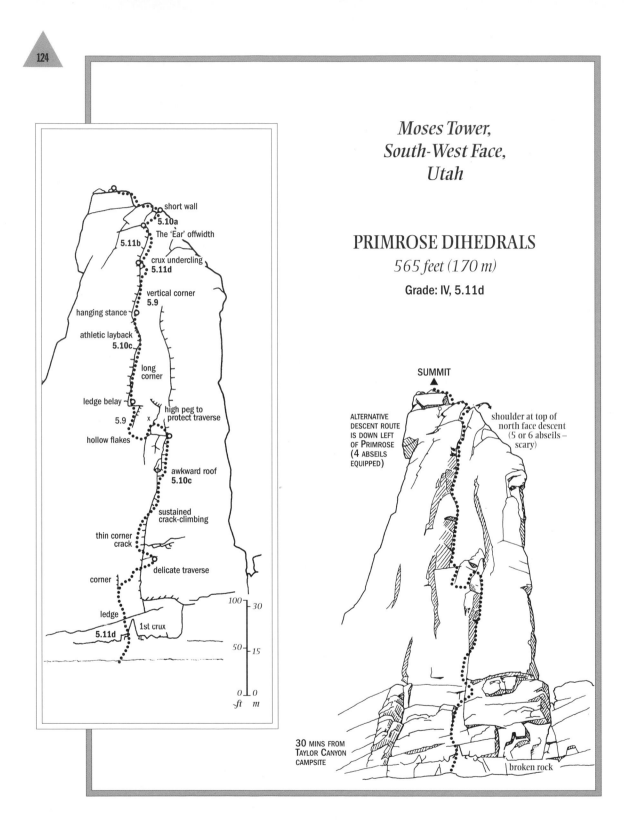

Moses Tower,
South-West Face,
Utah

PRIMROSE DIHEDRALS

565 feet (170 m)

Grade: IV, 5.11d

short wall
5.10a
The 'Ear' offwidth
5.11b
crux undercling
5.11d
vertical corner
5.9
hanging stance
athletic layback
5.10c
long corner
ledge belay
5.9   high peg to
   x   protect traverse
hollow flakes
awkward roof
5.10c
sustained crack-climbing
thin corner crack
delicate traverse
corner
ledge
5.11d   1st crux

100   30
50   15
0   0
ft   m

SUMMIT

ALTERNATIVE
DESCENT ROUTE
IS DOWN LEFT
OF PRIMROSE
(4 ABSEILS
EQUIPPED)

shoulder at top of
north face descent
(5 or 6 abseils –
scary)

30 MINS FROM
TAYLOR CANYON
CAMPSITE

broken rock

be confusing, with sets of rules to be negotiated. Booking as far in advance as possible is the easiest option but exact dates have to be given and the number in the party specified, together with the means of transport. Only four-by-four vehicles are allowed on the park's dirt tracks; all permits must be collected on arrival and appropriate fees paid. Numbers are strictly controlled and turning up at short notice in the holiday season and at weekends can result in being told that the park is, administratively at least, full and therefore being prevented from camping. This bureaucracy can test the patience, especially as the rules seem to change from year to year and the park staff have been in a long-running dispute with their state employers which has resulted in a work-to-rule.

Yet even a cursory visit to Canyonlands proves the hassle to be worthwhile. Here over 300,000 acres (121,405 hectares) of remote landscape typify Utah's canyon country as portrayed in innumerable B-movie Westerns and cigarette commercials. Even collecting permits from The Island in the Sky Visitor Center allows a glimpse east into the depths of the Shafer Canyon, where the steeply eroded sides drop almost sheer to the floor over 1500 feet (457 m) below. The journey to Moses Tower reinforces this large-scale picture and underlines Canyonlands as the most remote of Utah's national parks. Driving only 40 miles (64 km) along the dirt roads takes nearly two hours and shows much of the park's scenic variety, the most spectacular moments being a steep multi-hairpin descent from the high-level plateau to the evocatively named Horsethief Bottom and the meandering Green River. Aid and Airlie spent time looking at the climbing possibilities on the walls opposite, which helped to detract their attention from the track forced precariously between steep crag faces and a 50-foot (15-m) drop to the river below. Moses Tower is hidden until almost the end of the drive and is not seen until 2$\frac{1}{2}$ miles (4 km) up the Taylor Canyon. At the track's end a primitive campsite (where a chemical toilet is the only facility) gives a splendid close-up view of the Tower and its smaller neighbours, Zeus and Aphrodite. Guarding the surrounding landscape like lone sentinels, they look most striking in the evening when the fading light adds a warm brilliance to their already red hue.

Aid and Airlie set about establishing a camp and checking that they had remembered everything, for here even water must be brought in. While Airlie unpacked the car, Aid made sure that the growlers (which he had somehow found

Airlie struggling to gain height on the crux first pitch of Primrose Dihedrals on Moses Tower.
Most of the climbing is via cracks but here the only holds are tiny edges.

Aid attempting to move onto the first belay stance. Although the handholds are good, there are virtually
no footholds, necessitating a strenuous swing to the right.

time to fill overnight in Moab with a variety of different beers) had survived the journey intact. They cooked a quick meal, sorted out their gear for an early start the following morning, and tested the quality of the beer.

Early the next day, after half an hour's walk Aid and Airlie reached the base of Moses and then skirted below the awesome south-west face. Smooth shields of red, ochre and black rock soared 600 feet (183 m) vertically above. Etched into this sandstone bastion were flawless cracks as straight as rulers, clean-cut corners of improbable beauty, and near the summit jutted overhangs that somehow defied gravity. Towards the right side of the slender face they stopped by a cluster of primroses, which somehow managed to survive the arid sand and rock environment;

OVERVIEW OF DESERT CLIMBING

The Colorado Plateau stretches 16,000 square miles (41,440 square km) through Utah, Arizona, New Mexico and Colorado. It is a vast area of sedimentary sandstone wherein lies the greatest potential for desert-climbing in the world. The rock quality is variable, and most of the climbing is on the harder Wingate sandstone walls. Even the best sandstones are soft and smooth, and as a result desert-climbs invariably follow cracks.

The centre of desert-climbing is the lively town of Moab, as the best and most developed areas are to be found nearby in Canyonlands National Park, Castle Valley, Fisher Towers, Arches National Park, Potash Road and Indian Creek. The other main area is Zion National Park to the west. *Desert Rock* by Eric Bjørnstad is a good guide that describes the climbs in these areas.

Because of the obviously hot desert climate, the best times to climb are in early spring and late autumn. Winter is OK on south-facing routes but can be surprisingly cold in the shade.

Because of the soft nature of the rock, extreme caution must be used when climbing. Protection and belays cannot be taken for granted and it is recommended that experience is gained on shorter routes before a major tower is attempted.

Many of the climbing areas are in national parks, and permits are sometimes required to climb and camp. In addition, a very strong environmental policy is pursued, and all new bolts and pegs are banned. Use of chalk is also discouraged. The desert is a fragile place where refuse will lie for years and cryptobiotic soil can be destroyed just by walking on it. Keep to the trails and take all litter out with you.

above, where two walls met a continuous series of eye-catching corners like an open book, defined their intended climb – Primrose Dihedrals.

The first ascent of Primrose Dihedrals in April 1979 by Ed Webster, over two days solo, was considered a breakthrough in desert climbing and graded 5.8, A3 in difficulty. Yet, not satisfied with the artificial aids he used on the first ascent, Webster returned with Steve Hong in October of the same year and free-climbed the route at 5.11d in difficulty, creating a stunning climb.

In quiet anticipation Aid and Airlie emptied their rucksacks and started preparing for the climb. First they taped their hands with white zinc oxide tape to form a fingerless glove to protect their skin in preparation for jamming their hands in cracks, a technique repeated constantly and essential for desert-climbing where often the only holds are smooth-sided cracks. Then they sorted out their protection gear, carefully racking each piece on their harness or bandoleer so it would be readily accessible when they climbed.

To protect their climb up the smooth cracks they had to rely on special camming devices, often called 'cams' or 'friends', numerically sized to indicate the width of the crack. Before their invention almost 20 years ago free-climbing in the desert was virtually impractical.

'How many number 3 friends should we take?' Airlie asked.

'I guess three, as long as we take a couple of 2^1/2s and 3^1/2s,' Aid replied.

'I won't be able to climb with all this weight!' Airlie exclaimed.

'Yeah, it's a problem with desert-climbing. You need a huge rack. The pitches are so long, and often the cracks are the same size all the way!' Aid explained, aware that Airlie had never climbed in the desert.

'Better carry a bit extra weight and be safe,' he added, reinforcing his safety-first attitude to climbing.

Finally they were ready to go, and Aid quickly climbed 10 feet (3 m) into a deceptively easy-looking shallow inverted-V slot, which from the ground looked as though bridging and chimneying techniques would soon solve the difficulties described in the guidebook as the technical (5.11d) crux of the climb. Soon Aid realized why it was graded so highly in difficulty as he searched in vain for adequate holds on the impending wall. There were none, and so by ingeniously pressing one leg behind and the other in front, like a hurdler caught in mid-stride, and using his

height advantage, his fingers just reached a horizontal break. Above there was no rest, and the only protection was in a loose flake.

'Watch the rope Airlie. My arms are getting pumped. It's steeper than it looks,' Aid shouted.

It was not the ideal start to a climb as there was no time to warm up or get used to the uncompromising style of desert-climbing. Three days ago it was crampons and ice axes; now it was rock shoes and taped hands. A couple of insecure layback moves and Aid was relieved to reach easier ground that soon led to the first belay ledge. He was pleased to have fired off the hard moves first time, a great boost to his confidence.

Although Airlie is a powerful climber who has done several rock routes in Derbyshire way beyond Aid's comprehension, she lacked his height and, try as she might, she could not reach the crucial holds in the break. She tired rapidly as she strained repeatedly to gain height – not a good omen on the first few feet of a 600-foot (183-m) tower! Swearing profusely, Airlie was lowered to the ground. Rock-climbing was meant to be her forte, and here she was back on the ground, depressed and under pressure to climb. She had to find a way of reaching the break which was not height-dependent.

'Keep the rope tight, Aid. I'm going to try using the pocket on the right.'

With her boots smearing on the smooth wall, she pulled with all her strength and reached the holds above. By the time she reached the belay she was not confident about continuing.

Now it was Airlie's turn to lead and when all the gear was racked, her earlier fears were confirmed. 'I can't climb with this bloody weight round my neck, I can hardly move!' Airlie said in a stroppy voice, more to herself than to Aid.

Aid was starting to get used to Airlie's self-inquisitions and made no comment.

A tricky traverse led to the start of the crack, which soared skywards 120 feet (36 m) without a ledge for rest and virtually no footholds to help progress. It was typical of difficult desert-climbing, but Airlie was not accustomed to such continuous and sustained crack-climbing. Daunted by what lay above, she hand-jammed and

Half-way up the slender Moses Tower. Aid can be seen leading the third pitch with Airlie hanging from her belay. The route follows the corners (or dihedrals) above and below the climbers.

laybacked the first part of the crack, which lay in a left-facing corner. Placing protection at regular intervals, she made steady progress until she had to balance rightwards and layback in the opposite direction.

'Oh no! Bloody cracks. Hell! No! *No! No!* I'm off. Watch me. I'm coming off.'

Out of sight, Aid tensed and gathered in any slack rope ready for the fall. All he heard was Airlie's swearing, then silence, then scraping and the clanking of gear.

'Come on. No! I can't do it. Yes! Give me some rope. Quick. Yes! Oh, no!' Airlie argued with herself.

Meanwhile Aid was getting a little confused as to whether Airlie was climbing, falling or stuck. Most people when they are having a battle bottle up their feelings, but Airlie gave the world a running commentary on her emotions, usually in graphic swearwords.

'Fuck, fuck – this is desperate. I'm off. OK. Come on, you can do it,' she continued.

Initially, Aid thought Airlie would not get up the pitch, but soon he got the idea that this was Airlie's way of climbing. A few feet of climbing then a pause, followed by: 'Oh, shit. Shit! No. Oh, this hurts. I can't do it. Fucking gear!'

Then more upward movement. The higher she got, the more explicit the language. With as much self-doubt as she could muster, and with the help of every swearword related to male and female anatomy, sado-masochism and the sexual encounters of deviants, Airlie arrived at the top of the second pitch.

Aid followed with trepidation after Airlie's battle, but soon he found he could get reasonable jams in the crack and use his feet to take the strain. With confidence he reached the hanging stance, where Airlie was still having doubts about whether she could continue.

'I thought it was bloody hard. I laybacked most of it,' Airlie said. Then dejectedly: 'I can't jam that well.'

Aid replied: 'I found it hard as well, but at least I jammed it. It must have been desperate laybacking it!'

Then, thinking that Airlie was having a bit of a hard time, he added 'I'll lead the next few pitches until you get your confidence back.' This made Airlie even more frustrated with herself and she commented later: 'I was shocked to have found it hard, but I knew it wasn't that hard. I just couldn't see how to do it.

I spend all winter on climbing walls and then climb on limestone most times outside. I'm not used to the struggle of crack-climbing. I suppose if I act like an incompetent I should be treated like one!'

The third rope length traversed left to a ledge at the start of the main corner system, which cut through the surrounding monolithic walls all the way to the summit. The ledge was one of the few on the climb and was the excuse for a break and a drink. Even though it was the beginning of March they were full in the sun and the temperature was in the high 20s. That, and the dry desert air and their exertions, made for thirsty work.

Conscious that it was now early afternoon, Aid continued up the long corner above. It looked every bit as hard as the climbing below, but luckily in the back was a crack perfect for hand-jamming. Half-way up he was stopped by a square-cut overhang, but the holds were good and it provided strenuous entertainment rather than any great difficulty.

'I'm at the belay, Airlie, but there's no ledge. It will have to be a hanging stance,' Aid shouted.

While he belayed Airlie up the next pitch, he thought about her attitude to him. At 22 he had been a bit like her: pretty wild, outspoken, dedicated to what he was doing, with no money and living in poor conditions. Things hadn't changed that much for young climbers in a generation. But since moving to the States he'd noticed a big difference in attitudes between men and women, not just in climbing but in life in general. He often climbed with girls in the USA and felt them to be totally equal, trusting their decisions and respecting their ability. The equal relationship between climbers of both sexes was taken for granted in the States. That had not been the case back in Britain 20 years ago, and he suspected was still not the case now by Airlie's confrontational attitude. He thought she was striving to find her identity as a woman above her male counterparts and seemed to see men as a threat – dangerous and dominant. From what he gathered from Airlie, she climbed with her girlfriends back in Britain as a statement and because she preferred it, which he thought was symptomatic of the historical cultural divide between the sexes in Britain. A couple of months in the States would soon change her attitudes, he mused.

Airlie found the pitch hard, but when she reached the belay she was in a much more relaxed and positive frame of mind.

'I'll lead up to the Ear,' she said and set off up the steep rock.

Climbing positively, she soon completed the pitch.

'The next pitch looks wild! Hang on a bit while I get some good bomber gear in the belay,' she shouted.

When Aid reached the stance they had to organize themselves methodically. One false move and the consequences would be terminal, as they dangled 400 feet (122 m) above the ground, suspended only from one fixed bolt and the pieces of protection Airlie had managed to place in the surrounding soft and friable sandstone.

Aid took his time preparing for the next section of the climb – the infamous 'Ear', which aptly described the large flake of rock protruding out of the corner system. Although not graded as hard as the first pitch, it had the reputation of being a desperate struggle and the psychological crux of the climb.

'Climb the Ear via 5.11+ offwidth (eight inch). A transition is made to a few lieback moves which widen to a tight squeeze chimney then a sloping belay ledge.' The guidebook so describes climbing the Ear, but in practice they had to perform these gymnastics by traversing above a sheer wall that dropped straight to the ground with exposure similar to hanging from their fingertips off the top of the Eiffel Tower.

When Ed Webster was faced with this impasse on the first ascent he hand-drilled holes in the soft rock and placed in them a series of small bolts, which he used as aids to overcome the obstacle. When he returned with Steve Hong, they managed to climb the Ear in better style without pulling on the bolts, so making the first 'free' ascent.

'Watch me carefully, Airlie. I'll go up and see if I can climb it without the bolts,' Aid said without a great deal of conviction.

A few moves up and Aid's confidence started to evaporate. He looked back at Airlie hanging in mid-air and at the exposure below him. By wedging his shoulder in the crack which was too big for his hands but not big enough for his body (perversely called an offwidth crack), he managed to make some progress. Then a transition had to be made by strenuously pulling on the undercut lip of the Ear while smearing the feet on the holdless wall below.

'I can't make the move,' Aid said, more to himself than Airlie.

'Go on, Aid, give it a try,' encouraged Airlie.

▶ Aid and Airlie triumphant on the top of 600-foot (183-m) Moses Tower.

'No. Watch me! No. I'm going to have to use the bolts. I don't want to take a flyer on to those shitty old bolts!' Aid resigned himself almost with relief.

Once he had used one bolt he reasoned he might as well use the lot; most people who climbed Primrose used their aid. So carefully he used the next four bolts first by clipping a krab attached to a sling into the bolt and then gently standing in the sling, not wanting to put too much force on the 20-year-old bolts. This led him under the Ear and around to the smooth vertical chimney on the right. Here there were no more bolts and Aid had to wedge his body in the crack and squirm up the fissure. The effort required to move upwards was phenomenal, as his body, wedged so that it would not fall, created resistance to upward movement. Aid reached the sloping belay ledge exhausted.

Airlie made a valiant effort to second the Ear without using the bolts. In fact, she made the difficult first moves, but then her strength gave out and she fell onto

RECOMMENDED DESERT ROUTES

The best climbing can be divided into regions, often defined by national parks.

Castle Valley: The Kor–Ingalls (III 5.9) on Castleton Tower is the most popular tower route and a great introduction to desert-climbing. Fine Jade (III 5.11a) on the Rectory is also excellent.

Canyonlands National Park: Primrose Dihedrals (IV 5.11d) on Moses Tower is a must.

Fisher Towers: From a distance these towers look fantastic, but at close quarters they consist of vertical dirt. They are extremely challenging and are for the experienced. The Finger of Fate (V 5.9 A2+) on The Titan is the time-tested mud classic.

Indian Creek: This area is world famous for single-pitch crack climbs on perfect sandstone escarpments. There are hundreds of routes but start with Incredible Hand Crack (5.10), Super Crack (5.10) and The Wave (5.11). Further down the valley, Lightning Bolt Crack (III 5.11) on North Six Shooter is one of the finest tower routes in the desert.

Zion National Park: The challenges here are big walls up to 2000 feet (610m) for the experienced climber. The routes fill a guidebook, but some of the best are Monkey Finger Wall (IV 5.12 or 5.9 C2 where the C grade indicates hammerless aid climbing), Space Shot (V 5.7 C2), Moonlight Buttress (V 5.13 or 5.9 C1) and Touchstone Wall (IV+ 5.9 C1). There are plenty of shorter routes, for example at the base of Touchstone Wall.

Moab: This town is the best base for desert-climbing, offering plenty of climbing on escarpments around the town, in particular Heat Wave Wall and the sport climbing on Potash Road.

the rope. After a rest on the rope she continued into the squeeze chimney. This was not anatomically designed for women but, eventually, cursing and swearing, she pulled on to the ledge to join Aid.

Airlie asked Aid: 'Why didn't you try to free the pitch? You wouldn't have come to any harm falling.'

Aid looked perplexed. 'I never fall off. That's my philosophy.'

Airlie was shocked. 'You never fall off…Jesus! I fall off all the time. You can't be trying hard enough!'

The last two easier pitches were an anticlimax after the hard climbing below, but when Airlie finally pulled on to the 12-foot-square (3$\frac{1}{2}$-m-square), flat summit the view was breathtaking. The late-afternoon sun was turning the surrounding desert mesa and butte landscape beautiful ochre and red pastel shades, and in the shadows clung white patches of snow deposited by the same storm that had hit Santaquin a week earlier. Far below, the only evidence of man was the little dirt road that snaked to their campsite in the base of Taylor Canyon. Time has little meaning in this landscape, and their tents could easily have been a group of Indian tepees. Airlie was very reflective on reaching the summit:

I wish I'd done more of that type of climbing so I could have appreciated and enjoyed it more. It was memorable and a real struggle, but I don't really feel satisfied or happy inside myself because I didn't perform well on the climb. I found it harder than I expected and fell off a couple of times. In the type of sports climbing I normally do, if you fall you have failed, but I guess this is different as the summit is important and so it's more like mountaineering.

Aid asked: 'Would it have been a better experience if you had done it with a girl-friend rather than a man twice your age?'

Airlie's answer was expected. 'It would have been better, but I have lots of older friends and climbing cuts through age barriers. Anyway, you weren't too patronizing or paternal!'

Under a stone on the summit was a small tin box, inside which was a book with a record of the privileged few who had climbed Moses. Aid and Airlie filled in their names and then turned to organize their ropes for the abseil descent.

Pabbay, Scotland

5

'Do we really have to do this?'

Dave Cuthbertson, universally known simply as 'Cubby', was gazing at a sheep that was still just alive but had already lost one of its eyes to scavenging birds. Despite an inshore breeze, the stench was appalling and a putrefying liquid was oozing out of its stomach. After a journey by ferry from Oban, on Scotland's west coast, to the island of Barra, Cubby and his long-time friend Brian Hall had joined a sightseeing trip around the group of islands that make up the very southernmost tip of the Outer Hebrides with a request to be dropped ashore on the small uninhabited island of Pabbay. For Cubby this was not a tourist jaunt but the serious business of investigating the potential for a hard new route on the Great Arch, which is on the west coast of Pabbay and takes the full force of the pounding Atlantic Ocean. Lynn Hill, America's leading female climber, was not due for another week or more, and in the interim decisions would need

Dave (Cubby) Cuthbertson makes a long reach over the black basalt dyke overhang and finds the crucial small hold which solved this difficult section on the third pitch of the Great Arch.

to be made, but the trip had not got off to an auspicious start. Psyched up to investigate a new route, Cubby was now diverted into pulling the sheep from the only stream that provided a good source of drinking water before he could begin to think about any climbing. It was not an appealing prospect and Cubby undertook it out of necessity, not willingness.

Dave Cuthbertson is arguably the best all-round climber that Scotland has ever produced. Born and brought up in a working-class household on the south side of Edinburgh, he struggled through a rough school where 'it was difficult for me to actually learn anything' but was already a keen climber by the time he left. Today, Cubby is still defensive about his education, often suggesting that he is not an intellectual and is someone who finds it hard to understand complex issues. In reality, the opposite is true: although his working-class roots go very deep and influence much of his thinking, he is sensitive and thoughtful and has a doggedly determined personality. Now approaching 40, he is 5 feet, 6 inches (1.67 m) tall, softly spoken and extremely conscious of his image and appearance. It is part of Cubby's complex make-up that he sometimes feels people take advantage of him, and in a group discussion he frequently believes that his voice goes unheard.

Few climbers have thought about their sport and their motivation as much as Dave has. He had initially found climbing 'quite scary' but his competitive nature meant that on his first day out he undertook a climb at the hardest grade of that time – VS (Very Severe). Looking back on that first route Cubby recalls that 'it was a very ignorant and a very dangerous thing to do' but also admits that the competitive streak was not the sole factor in his early climbing: 'It was also the adventure – seeing different places, being with different people, away from the city and being a mountaineer.' At first he did not think of himself as a natural climber and, like many novices, was attracted initially as much by the equipment as the climbing. Yet soon he realized that the immense enjoyment he got from climbing reflected a natural ability and today he freely admits that climbing dominates his life.

I don't like to think of it as an obsession, though I'm sure it is. At times I have to take some sort of control over it because it can run your life. After

25 years, climbing has taken such a grip of me that I still commit myself more to climbing than I can to work. So I work just enough to climb. That is quite deliberate. I kid myself at times and say that this is the year I'm going to start a business and make some money, but it never works out that way.

The result of this commitment to the sport is that Cubby finds difficulty in undertaking anything that might interfere with his climbing, and he is not, for example, someone who takes naturally to sponsorship, feeling that an obligation to a company might interfere with his plans. He is someone who can easily feel pressurized or appear prickly, whether this is related to any ambitious new route or just committing himself to fairly mundane travel arrangements. Yet watching him on the rock face is an entirely different experience. Although the days are gone when a climber could excel in every aspect of the sport, Cubby has come very near to achieving that. In the last few years he has concentrated on sport climbing but has done so having left an incredible mark on traditional climbing (both rock and ice) and having achieved creditable performances on the indoor competition circuit. Most recently he has returned to traditional climbing and has done a number of hard routes up to E8, as well as a grade IX mixed ice route in winter.

Cubby has put up something in the region of 300 new routes, but in his eyes it is not the sheer quantity that is significant. More importantly, he has tried to concentrate on lines of real quality. One such defining climb is Wild Country on the Cobbler in the Arrochar Alps, which he put up in 1979:

It was the first time where I had used bouldering techniques on a climb. I let myself go and climbed to my limit. Wild Country was a big step forward for me and for Scottish climbing. I wasn't sure what I was doing with my climbing until then. I wanted to be the best, I suppose.

▶ **The Great Arch.** The route starts just right of the small sea inlet and then climbs the buttress on the left to the narrowest part of the large lower overhang. The offwidth slot is then climbed into the corner above and then diagonally across the wall sandwiched between the upper and lower overhangs (climbers just visible). The top arched overhang is breached just before it goes out of picture.

Cubby's fascination for routes involving ever greater difficulty led him to make a seven-week attempt on a new line at the popular Dumbarton Rock, west of Glasgow. Requiem, as the climb was known, was generally thought to be the hardest route of its type and went unrepeated for no less than six years, although it coincides with what Cubby now thinks of as the one murky period in his climbing career. At the time he annoyed some of his rivals by abseiling down and aggressively cleaning the route and also, while placing pegs for protection, he inadvertently improved some of the holds. Even after adopting these tactics, which are not exceptional by modern standards, he still regards it as 'among the hardest routes in the world at that time'.

Similarly, Cubby was one of a number of élite climbers fascinated by the prospect of making a winter ascent of the classic summer rock route Guerdon Grooves in Glen Coe, first climbed by John Cunningham and Bill Smith in June 1948. It is a technically difficult and highly exposed line, and the prospect of

PABBAY'S CLIMBING HISTORY

Much written evidence exists about the climbing exploits of the natives from the outer Scottish Isles before the early part of this century. This is epitomized by people hunting seabirds and taking eggs by climbing the sea stacks around St Kilda, but some evidence suggests that this took place on Mingulay, the island closest to Pabbay.

Apart from a minor foray on the cliffs to the south of the beach in 1989, the first major climbing was in 1995 when two parties visited the island. The first was a party of Germans, who climbed about a dozen routes, in particular Spit in Paradise (E3) and U-Ei (HVS) on the Pink Walls. A group of Scots followed (K. Howett, G.E. Little, G. Nicoll and A. Cunningham), their most significant route being The Priest (E2) on Arch Wall. In 1996 a larger Scottish team, some of whose members had come the previous year, climbed 30 new routes, including one of the finest in the Outer Hebrides which the first ascensionists (Howett and Little) called Prophesy of Drowning (E3). The trend of a dozen climbers getting together and hiring a boat for a couple of weeks' climbing was continued in 1997 when many of the team from the year before visited the island, again climbing a number of excellent new routes.

attempting a winter ascent had attracted some of the best climbers of that time, including Alan Rouse, Kenny Spence, Murray Hamilton and Alan Taylor. In the winter of 1984 Dave, together with Arthur Paul, arrived in Glen Coe to make their attempt. They were worried when they discovered that Al Rouse had been there just a few days earlier to make his own attempt. Although Cubby was convinced that they had not made a successful ascent, he was nonetheless delighted when he found proof: 'I remember seeing the scuffs in the snow and was quite pleased to see they ran out a wee bit later on before they had reached the hard part of the climb.' After climbing most of the route – which left them extended on every pitch – Cubby and Arthur Paul were turned back just 30 feet (9 m) short of major difficulties when a big storm came in and fading daylight forced a hasty retreat. A week later, after the storm had abated and conditions improved, they returned to try again. On one of Scotland's most important first ascents, Cubby and Arthur Paul were able to claim the prize as theirs. Such is the ferocity of the route and the consequences of the leader taking a fall that even after numerous attempts, at the time of writing some 13 years later, it still awaits a second winter ascent.

His one disappointment has been that a brief foray into Himalayan climbing was unsuccessful. He was part of a strong team that planned to attempt the east face of Kedarnath in the Gangotri region of the Garhwal Himalayas in 1985. Unfortunately, Cubby picked up a virus in Delhi and by the fourth day of the trip was already feeling ill. On arrival at base camp he realized that his condition was worsening and that he needed to descend to a lower altitude. On the walk out Cubby met one of the other team members who recognized the tell-tale symptoms of pulmonary oedema. By now Cubby was in a comatose state. He passed out to wake up three days later in hospital, where he spent ten days and was ill for a considerable time after. Although he now knows that greater time would be needed to acclimatize, he has never returned to the Himalayas in spite of receiving invitations to join other expeditions. It was partly this experience that led him to concentrate on Scottish climbing – with such spectacular results.

His achievements in climbing competitions are also testimony to his ability. He first became a member of the British climbing team in the late 1980s when he was 31, but the other members were either teenagers or in their twenties. His high point came in that very first year, when he was placed tenth at Lyons; Cubby argues that this has particular significance. He claims that at that time he had no method to his training, yet when he had evolved his own system the standards had been raised even higher and remained elusively out of his reach. Cubby has also suffered from a number of injuries that have curtailed his activity, a torn ligament in his arm causing long-term problems. He last competed in the 1995–6 season; although highly motivated to win, the best he could manage was third overall in the British Championships. Many people might think this a creditable performance, but Cubby measures himself against the severest standards.

Yet at the heart of Cubby's climbing, for all its outstanding successes, there is, in some climbers' eyes, a contradiction. Part of his temperament is to play down the importance of what he has done but then to be frustrated, even upset, when that importance is not immediately recognized by others. While being a poor and reluctant self-publicist, he can be annoyed that others do not give him the recognition he clearly merits. He is outstanding on both rock and ice: an experienced alpinist and a professional mountain guide. His experience demonstrates an all-round ability that very few climbers can lay claim to. Cubby is also fiercely patriotic and takes it personally when Scotland is described, quite erroneously, as a climbing backwater, and he feels that being Scottish has resulted in not being accorded true recognition. So the notion of tackling a new route with one of the world's most important climbers on an uninhabited Scottish island was one that appealed to him.

Cubby and Lynn relax between attempts on the Arch.

Cubby had wanted to visit the southern Outer Hebrides for a long time, and although he is one of the authors of the Scottish Mountaineering Club *Climbers' Guide to Skye and the Hebrides* he did not write the section on the isles of Mingulay and Pabbay. But Cubby never goes anywhere without meticulous preparation and research, and armed with the information from the guides and a couple of articles from climbing magazines and from conversations with contemporaries who had visited the islands he had a detailed knowledge of the existing climbing, together with potential new routes, before he even stepped ashore.

The island is just over a mile square and its profile looks like a wedge of cheese. Treeless heather moorland rises from the beautiful white sands of the landing beach on the east side to the wind-swept high point of the Hoe at 561 feet (171 m) altitude on the west side before falling abruptly in a series of spectacular cliffs to the turbulent Atlantic below. On the reconnaissance Cubby and Brian took an hour to walk across the island to the top of the Hoe and quickly identified the descent to the base of the Great Arch, reputed to be one of the most spectacular cliffs in the whole of the Western Isles. In a country with a large and active climbing population, discovering a piece of virgin rock of this size and steepness was a rarity.

From the cliff top the Arch was hidden in the back of a zawn (a deep-incut bay or inlet) below, but the cliff was revealed as Cubby zigzagged down the steeply sloping grass and short rock steps that led to the wave-washed platforms above the sea. 'It looks a wee bit dark and dingy,' Cubby remarked with disappointment, adding: 'It's not as impressive as in the photos.' It was midday and the sun was just starting to hit the pillars of rock on the left of the Arch, turning the Lewisian gneiss a beautiful pastel red-brown highlighted by horizontally waved black basalt dykes and crystalline veins of white quartz. By contrast, the unlit Arch was black and dripping with water from recent rain. Certainly impressive but not very appealing to climb.

From the side Cubby identified the existing routes, the best of which was reputed to be Prophesy of Drowning, which climbed the pillars and corners to the left of the Great Arch. No climb took the main challenge of the Great Arch. He then clambered through the boulders at the base to gain a closer look.

Whereas the foot of the Arch could be reached even at high tide, the left-hand side of the cliff, where all the existing routes started, was isolated by a narrow inlet of sea.

Standing at the foot of the Arch was truly awesome, a feeling more associated with looking up at the roof inside a medieval cathedral. The action of the sea had undercut the 260-foot (80-m) wall, peeling off house-sized chunks of rock that now lay at the foot. The rock architecture that this violent erosion had left was a wall split by two huge overhanging roofs. The lower one formed a 25-foot (8-m) horizontal barrier across the whole wall 165 feet (50 m) from the base. The higher, 15-foot (5-m) overhang created the arch that capped the wall like a giant Gothic lintel, its apex curving to within a few yards of the top of the cliff. From below it looked impregnable, and certainly to break through the lower band of overhangs looked like a climb for future generations to tackle, but the top overhang was not as wide and at the very apex there seemed to be a crack splitting the rock. The only way to find out if it was climbable was to have a closer look.

Cubby and Brian retraced their steps to the top of the cliff and found a good anchor in rocks on a grass ledge directly above the apex of the arch. The 330 feet (100 m) of rope they attached to the anchor disappeared into space, not touching rock until it reached the boulders 45 feet (15 m) out from the base. 'It must be one of the most overhanging cliffs in Britain,' Cubby remarked. He attached his figure-of-eight abseiling device to the rope and started to descend. Brian paid out an additional safety rope, prudent for such a long abseil where the climber would not touch the rock.

At the lip of the overhang the sense of exposure was immediate and dramatic as the rope snaked through space to the ground far below. Even Cubby, a most experienced climber, felt a rush of adrenalin at the fear and vulnerability of such a situation, made more acute by the sudden transition from walking on *terra firma* to hanging in space. He carefully studied the overhang, which disappeared away from him, and was encouraged by what he saw. It was undoubtedly going to be desperate climbing just by the strenuous nature of hanging on while trying to cross the ceiling, but a series of flakes created a line of holds from the back of the overhang to within a body's length of the lip. This last section, then climbing around the lip on to the vertical wall above, looked very tricky indeed.

Cubby continued to descend the rope, now hanging totally free in space. Without being able to touch the rock he continually spun around, getting an alternate view of the cliff and then the sea. Disorientated and now hanging 45 feet (15 m) out from the face, he could not get a good look at the rock. However, he could see enough to confirm that the bottom overhang could not be breached by free-climbing (given the time available on the island) but where it merged into the corners and pillars on the left there could be a way of avoiding the widest part of the overhang to gain access to the upper wall sandwiched between the two overhangs. This upper wall could then be traversed to gain the apex of the Arch.

With the evening sun the Arch came to life, looking a different, friendlier place from when they had first arrived. Where before there were only sombre shadows, now the evening rays picked out the features and colours in the gneiss. With a plan in place, and inspired by the last views of the Arch, Cubby and Brian left Pabbay to await Lynn's arrival.

It is tempting to think that Lynn Hill could not be more different from Dave Cuthbertson. She has a world-wide reputation, she can choose her sponsors from an almost endless list, she is continually in demand for personal appearances and she has, among other more notable achievements, been invited for tea at the White House. Physically, Lynn is under 5 foot 2 inches (1.56 m) tall, has a slim build and is capable of repeatedly sustaining the most athletic movements on rock. She is usually photographed with a distinctive mane of chestnut-coloured hair that gives an impression of power and purpose. Therefore, it came as a shock when she arrived on Pabbay with her hair braided into cornrows. If she wished to travel without being recognized there could not be a better way. Just a few years younger than Cubby, Lynn was born in 1961 and brought up in California as one of a large family of four brothers and two sisters. She has always participated in sports, winning her first prize in a swimming contest at the age of seven; this was followed by numerous athletics and gymnastic trophies. A few years later, climbing attracted Lynn's attention, bringing together all her many interests (including a love of the outdoors which had developed on family camping holidays) and satisfying an ambitious streak.

Before long she started to gain a reputation by putting up new routes at Joshua Tree in the Californian desert, around Telluride, Colorado, and at Red Rocks outside Las Vegas. She also got noticed by other climbers when she did the north-west face of Half Dome in Yosemite National Park (which she climbed with her first boyfriend, Charlie Row) and The Shield on El Capitan, also in Yosemite. Her talent as a climber was obvious almost from the beginning, but Lynn also excelled in a host of other directions: in the early 1980s she took part in Survival of the Fittest, a spectacular combination of running, swimming, kayaking, abseiling and other activities, which she won for four successive years. But in a country as vast as the United States climbers were, at that time, often isolated by distance and different traditions and Lynn wanted to move on. In 1983 she transferred her biology course to the University of New York and headed east. Here she started climbing in the Shawangunk Mountains, a series of quartzite cliffs on the west rim of the Hudson river valley, where she put up a number of new routes. In 20 years of outstanding climbing with an arm's-length list of achievements, there are two that immediately stand out: her phenomenal success in climbing competitions and her epoch-making climbs on The Nose in Yosemite.

Lynn's impact on the climbing competition circuit was spectacular, although it was often clouded by controversy. She took part in the first European competition, second stage, at Bardonecchia in Italy and discovered immediately that behind-the-scenes politicking played an important part in the final outcome. Lynn was the only competitor who managed to complete the final route, but despite this notable success the organizers were pressurized by the French into changing the rules while the competition was still in progress to use a system based on accumulated points. Now, with the change in the rules, Lynn was in joint first place with France's most famous female climber, Catherine Destivelle. Faced with this new dilemma, the judges referred back to their respective times and, in doing so, awarded the title to Destivelle. Hill was angry at the outcome, saying it was both unfair and unsportsmanlike to change the rules and arguing that it appeared that politics lay behind the French climber's victory. It was not an auspicious start to the European competition and was a foretaste of what was to come on a circuit that can sometimes be full of jealousy and nationalism.

Looking south from Pabbay across the sea to Mingulay. Ancient ruins are evident in the foreground.

As her success in competitions grew, Lynn alternated between the States and Europe and competed in both continents. Eventually, she decided to settle in France, where she lived until 1996. An intense rivalry developed between her and the more flamboyant Destivelle, but in 1990 she finished the season as joint winner of the World Cup. This time she tied with another high-profile French woman – Isabelle Patissier – and again her victory was no less controversial. At the event in Lyons she was preparing for a super-final between herself and Patissier which was on the same route used for the men's final. Walking into the isolation room she was stunned to find one of the French men explaining the details of the route to Isabelle. Insulted at what she saw as cheating, she set out into the arena and with terrific ability she climbed the route with total determination. Only two of the male finalists had accomplished such a feat, and her satisfaction was complete when she overheard Patissier had failed on the route and fallen off. However, she needed to win this event and the following one at Barcelona in order to tie with Patissier. The rules stated that only the best five results of the year counted, and when Lynn also won in Barcelona there was a dead heat in sight. Now French officials tried to get this rule waived so that their contestant would emerge as the outright winner. As a final twist Patissier left the auditorium before the awards ceremony and Hill stood alone on the podium. In the five years between 1987 and 1992, Lynn Hill was the most successful female competition climber in the world and, to give just one example, she won the Rockmaster International Championship at Arco in Italy no fewer than five times.

In 1993, and having retired from the world of climbing competitions, Hill undertook her next big project. She had a bold plan to free-climb one of the world's best-known multi-pitch rock routes in the world – The Nose on El Capitan in Yosemite. Up until her ascent, artificial aid had been used on the most difficult sections of the climb. Initially, she attempted this 34-pitch marathon with the British climber, and former World Cup champion, Simon Nadin. The 21 pitches leading up to the Great Roof had been harder than they had anticipated, but the roof itself was one of the major obstacles that needed to be overcome. Nadin failed in his attempt and handed over the lead to Hill, judging that she was more likely to succeed on the tiny underclings. Afterwards, writing in the magazine *On the Edge*, Nadin recalled: 'Dejected that I had failed at the first obstacle, the consolation of just doing The Nose wasn't enough. Lynn's free ascent of this pitch was inspirational. She had been on the edge, feet popping several times, but somehow summoning up enough reserves to complete it.'

After this, Hill and Nadin completed the climb, but they had failed to free-climb 5 feet (1.5 m) of one pitch. With success so close, Lynn was back two weeks later, this time in the company of Brooke Sandahl (who had also been trying to free-climb the route) and, taking a slightly different line on one pitch, she completed the entire route in four days. It was, as the American magazine *Climbing* noted, a route that 'required every technique in the book, from fingers to offwidth, and all different styles of face-climbing'.

As if this were not proof enough of her ability, Hill returned just over a year later, in the autumn of 1994, to make the second free ascent, but now she had another goal in mind – to climb this traditional multi-day route in under 24 hours. She teamed up with Steve Sutton, who jumared up behind her and held the ropes so that Lynn had no distractions from the actual climbing. With methodical thoroughness that routes like this demand, Lynn had worked out every minute detail of the climb, including the best time to start on the route. Accordingly, the pair set off at 10 p.m. and climbed throughout the night with the aid of headtorches. This time Lynn flashed every pitch except one and completed the whole route in 23 hours on 19 and 20 September. The attempt was full of drama none the less. On the evening of the 20th she failed on her first three attempts of the Great Dihedral before she successfully completed the pitch. For Hill this marked the culmination of her climbing career, but it is also an important landmark in the American history of the sport. Another American climber, Scott Franklin, had also worked on freeing the route and described Lynn's achievement succinctly: 'You probably won't see that getting done again anytime soon'.

Since her success on The Nose, Lynn has committed herself with breathtaking energy to a number of projects, including working on a book about her life and climbing, editing a film based on the ascent of The Nose, giving numerous public lectures and, of course, more climbing. With a hectic schedule spanning two continents, her time on Pabbay would be limited, but that did not diminish her excitement about a first climbing trip to Scotland.

When Lynn first saw the Great Arch on 11 June it was a cold and cloudy day and she reacted in a similar way to Cubby. 'It looks wet,' was her polite, jetlagged way of saying, 'Why the hell have I been brought half-way round the world to this piece of trash?' More at home on the perfect limestone of Provence or the rough granite of California, she had every right to question her sanity. During the day Cubby pointed out the various features of the wall and discussed a plan of 'attack', and by afternoon, when the sun came out and lit the Arch golden, she was much more positive about the project.

Before any attempt on the climb could be made, Cubby wanted Lynn to have a closer look by abseiling down the face, just as he had done on the reconnaissance. They would then have similar knowledge of the Arch and they could discuss the project on equal terms.

Next morning Cubby and Lynn walked from their campsite on the east side of the island across the windswept moors to the top of the Arch. When Lynn abseiled down the route she was impressed by the steepness and was sceptical about their ability to free-climb the route in the five days available but she concurred with Cubby's idea of breaking through the lower overhang at the left-hand side. Their major problem and crux of the route would be crossing the upper overhang at the apex of the Arch, which they would have to inspect, clean and possibly pre-place protection before they could even consider attempting to climb. It was not worth starting the bottom part of the Arch, which they felt sure they could do 'on sight' (without inspecting, cleaning or pre-placing protection), until they had confirmed the feasibility of the upper overhang. Their fear was that, after a detailed inspection, they would find it impossible to climb.

To gain access to the underside of the upper overhang was a very difficult operation that had to be done from the top, down, in the reverse direction to the one in which it would eventually be climbed. First, Cubby abseiled to the lip of the overhang and then used artificial aid to climb under the overhang. Strenuous progress was made by swinging virtually upside-down from the etriers, moving

Looking up the lower buttress, with climbers on the third pitch. The lead climber is approaching the black dyke overhang. Where the buttress hits the lower large overhang, the offwidth slot gives access to the wall sandwiched between the two overhangs.

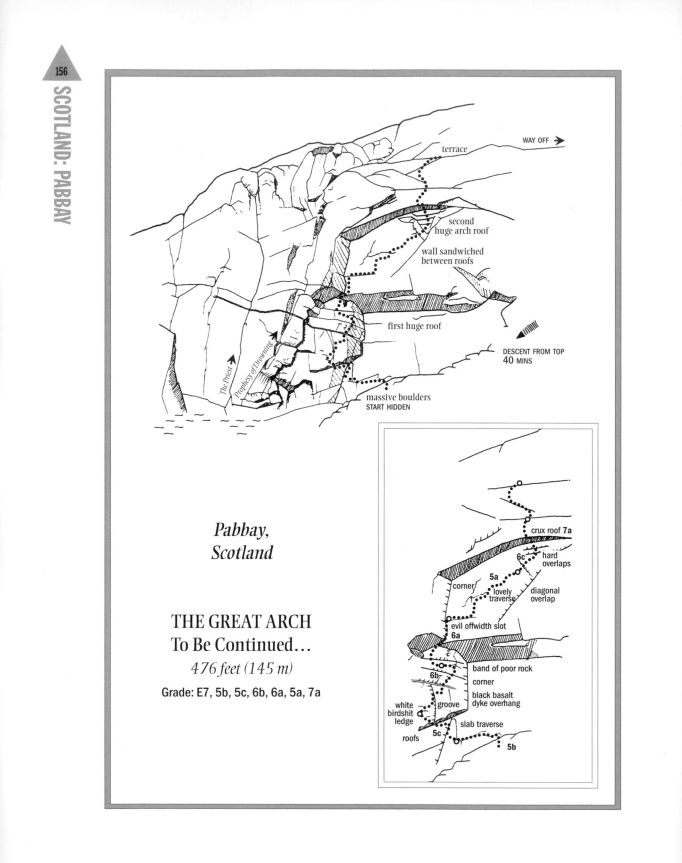

WAY OFF →

terrace

second
huge arch roof

wall sandwiched
between roofs

first huge roof

DESCENT FROM TOP
40 MINS

The Priest

Prophesy of Drowning

massive boulders
START HIDDEN

*Pabbay,
Scotland*

THE GREAT ARCH
To Be Continued…
476 feet (145 m)
Grade: E7, 5b, 5c, 6b, 6a, 5a, 7a

crux roof **7a**

6c hard
overlaps

5a
lovely
traverse

diagonal
overlap

corner

evil offwidth slot
6a

band of poor rock

6b
corner

black basalt
dyke overhang

white
birdshit
ledge

groove

slab traverse

roofs
5c

5b

from one piece of gear to the next, until the back wall of the overhang could be reached. Then a couple of small stepped overhangs below had to be contended with before he reached the easier vertical wall and a small ledge that could be used for a belay. The rope that he then fixed from the belay to the top of the cliff gave them access to work on the overhang under the Arch.

Lynn expressed her thoughts:

Really it makes sense to put some bolts in the top pitch, but I understand the problems over here. Because Britain is a relatively small country and the rock is a limited resource, it makes sense to covert first ascents and have strict traditional rules about bolting. I climbed in the Gunks [Shawangunks] on the east coast of the States for eight years, and the rock is quite similar to a lot of British rock and we had similar traditions. You had to earn a first ascent.

Cubby's reply was more an apology to Lynn about the state of British climbing than his own personal ethic:

What we have is a route of two halves, a hybrid between traditional adventure climbing at the bottom and modern sport climbing on the top pitch. If we were sensible, I agree, we would put a line of bolts across the top roof. What we are planning is to place lots of marginal nuts, pegs and friends instead of bolts to try to make it safe, but it's still going to be very intimidating to climb. It's going to be a mess and some of those flakes could be loose. I think British climbing is tying itself in a knot but we have to avoid using bolts because the ethical implications are a minefield and could set a precedent for other climbers to follow. People who stir the issue usually have no idea or experience like you or me. It annoys me that it's too easy doing things for other people rather than yourself, though it is good to be conscientious and think about your actions.

Over the next day Cubby and Lynn cleaned the rock of lichen and dirt with a wire brush. It was obvious that this top pitch was going to be very hard indeed, and they would not have enough strength to place all the protection while they were

hanging on under the overhang. With this in mind, Cubby pre-placed some essential protection, an accepted practice on such difficult climbs, but left the majority of the protection to be strenuously placed later when they came to lead the pitch. With the roof prepared, they were more confident of success and decided they should turn their attention to the lower part of the climb.

An unusual feature of the rock was that it appeared to ooze moisture when it was in the shade. This gave the rock a slippery texture totally unsuitable for high-grade climbing. By early afternoon the sun hit the face and within an hour the rock was dry. This unforeseen problem could have marked the end of their climbing had it not been for the excellent weather and the fact that it remained light until 11 p.m., allowing sufficient time for progress to be made even with a late start.

The buttress up which they hoped to start the climb was in the back left-hand corner of the zawn, isolated from access by an inlet of choppy sea washing over kelp and barnacle-covered boulders. To gain the bottom of the buttress, Lynn led an introductory pitch that traversed above the sea. Cubby soon joined Lynn on the stance and took over the lead. 'I'll take a look over there, across the wall under the overhang. I can't see the next bit too well, but I'll aim for the big ledge covered in white birdshit in the middle of the buttress,' he said while pointing at his plan of attack. A couple of large grey seals bobbed up and down in the sea below, their heads just out of the water and big round eyes looking up at the climbers in a bemused though wary kind of way. As soon as Cubby started to climb, courage deserted them and they somersaulted into the depths, reappearing further out to sea, still looking inquisitively.

A horizontal crack provided a handrail across the wall under the overhang. Even so, the wall was steep and to avoid using too much energy Cubby carefully positioned his feet to take his weight from his arms. All climbers have a different 'signature', a particular way in which they climb rock, and Cubby has a particularly distinctive style. His body is never still. Hands are continually searching for better holds, legs are always changing position to find the best

Looking up at Lynn attempting the black basalt dyke overhang. She fell off soon after and Cubby then found the key hold by climbing slightly right (see picture page 138). The overhanging nature of the cliff is all too apparent and the dark offwidth slot can be seen breaking through the overhangs above.

point of balance and to make sure that no muscle is stressed for any length of time. In his characteristic way he reached the end of the horizontal crack and now had to make a series of blind moves into the groove above. He placed a good runner and rested, then, with an explosive, though exact movement, he pulled into the groove above and soon reached the belay ledge, which he shared with a group of wary puffins and guillemots.

Lynn seconded the pitch (graded E3 5c by Cubby) without too much difficulty and then sorted out the gear, ready to lead the next pitch. The plan was to alternate the leading: in this way they would both contribute equally to the ascent. Both respected each other's ability and thought it vital to share the effort.

The buttress had looked an amenable angle from a distance, but that was certainly an optical illusion caused by comparing it with the surrounding huge overhangs. From the belay the buttress overhung considerably, and, 50 feet (15 m) above, a black basalt dyke formed an overhanging roof. To reach the dyke Lynn climbed a beautiful groove.

Her style of climbing was obviously very different from Cubby's. She explained:

I'm interested in body dynamics. Being small, I have to use my feet in intuitive ways as I can't make the spans of taller people. I try to get my feet high so I'm not stretched out. When I'm working a route I like to touch all the holds and try them in different combinations. I've been climbing 22 years so I know what sorts of positions are going to be useful, especially using my feet in opposition to take weight off my arms. Then there is the intuitive side which comes from the centre and is really body awareness or what feels in balance. Sometimes you have to shut down the brain after you have done the analysis and let the body shift into the right position. Finally, you have to know what you have done and remember so you can repeat all this!

At the black dyke overhang Lynn was stopped by a sudden increase in difficulty. She had two choices. A short, sharp and unprotected swing over the body length of roof directly above, which would be a case of all or nothing – success if there were holds, failure and a fall if she found nothing. A very bold prospect! Alternatively, she could see a line of good holds crossing the overhang on the left and a horizontal crack for protection. At the lip she could see a block, but the top of it sloped and she could not see if it would provide a hold. Leading 'on sight' is much harder and more unpredictable than when climbers inspect the route beforehand. Cubby and Lynn had not inspected this part of the route on purpose, wanting to experience the adventure and unknown element of the exploit. The downside was now all too apparent, as Lynn mused on her options and wondered if there was a hold above the overhang.

Prudently, she decided on going left and reached for the line of holds created at the junction of the gneiss and the black basalt. Immediately, she was hanging from her arms, so to relieve the strain she brought her feet up to the same level as her hands and heel-hooked them in the horizontal holds, like a sloth climbing a tree branch. There was a lot of rock debris on the holds and in this strenuous position she had to clean the holds and then place protection while she climbed. At the lip she was exhausted and quite a long way from her last runner, facing a nasty backwards fall. Sensibly, she did not commit to the difficult moves ahead; instead she scuttled back to her resting position at the top of the groove.

After five minutes' rest she climbed back to her high point and continued to the lip of the overhang. With power that belied her size, she pulled up and pivoted on her foot, at the same time reaching above. On her first try she found nothing; on her second try, and with an extra effort, she reached higher for a small wrinkle in the rock. It was nothing. A fall was certain if she could not make the move. Exhausted, she tried again. More desperate this time, she lurched up but again failed to make the move. Conscious that her last runners were some distance below and the swing from a fall could crash her into the rock, she made a frantic effort to retreat. Cubby, understanding the seriousness of her predicament, took in the rope as she climbed back under the overhang. She knew the fall was inevitable so she let her feet drop under control and, with all the weight coming on her worn-out arms, she fell. Cubby held the rope as she swung under the overhang then lowered her slowly down to the belay.

It was obvious that Lynn needed a long rest so Cubby took over the lead. He soon reached the black dyke overhang and, with the benefit of clean holds and the runners placed by Lynn, reached the lip relatively fresh. He then stretched right, and more by luck than planning found a small hidden fingerhold that proved to be the key to the move around the lip. A powerful, bold pull and a couple more stiff moves and Cubby was in balance on easier terrain. As he climbed higher through some poor-quality rock, the rope started to catch on the lip of the overhang. The rope drag finally became so bad that Cubby was forced to stop and belay.

Cubby thought the pitch warranted a hefty E5 or E6 grade. When Lynn seconded the pitch she still had trouble with the overhang. The key hold that had been just in reach for Cubby was out of reach for Lynn. Eventually with a long stretch she made the move and reached the belay, ready to lead the next pitch. Cubby was quite glad it was Lynn's turn as he had been eyeing with some trepidation the evil-looking overhanging chimney that was the only weakness breaking through the huge lower overhang.

On closer inspection it was more like an offwidth slot that split the 13-foot (4-m) overhang! Soon Lynn had climbed to below it and then spent some time arranging protection in the suspect and rotten rock in the back of the slot. She now used her size to her advantage as she managed to squirm totally inside the darkness. All Cubby could see was the soles of Lynn's shoes as she wriggled vulnerably outwards. There were virtually no holds and progress could be made only by jamming her whole body between the two walls of the slot. It felt very precarious but was probably just as difficult to fall off as it was to climb. Lynn remembers it vividly: 'It was a grunt, but the crucial move was trying to put my foot on this high foothold. It was so constricting I had to lift my foot and force it up and place it on the edge. It was a grovel-fest.'

By the time it was Cubby's turn to second the pitch he was cold and he had a torrid time. All who know Cubby well will have noticed that he has an attractive though prominent Roman nose. Unfortunately, he started the slot with his head facing left and soon found it had to face right. The slot was so constricting that the only way this could be done was to squash his nose flat against the rough rock, and even then he had barely enough room to turn his head. He was so involved with the manoeuvre that he did not notice the blood until later! To make matters worse,

Lynn working out the crux sequence on the upper overhang. The runner at the lip of the overhang is for protection only and was pre-placed by abseiling from the top.

being taller than Lynn caused all manner of problems: like a tall person in a short bed, his legs stuck out of the bottom. Unable to gain any purchase from his rock boots, he expended a huge amount of effort just to jam himself in the slot. To move he had to relax and un-jam himself, and as soon as he did so he felt as though he would come shooting out of the bottom of the slot, minus his nose and probably his head. Eventually, he followed Lynn's tactic and lifted his foot onto a crucial hold, then grovelled and scraped his way out of the bowels and reached Lynn in a rather dishevelled state, very impressed at her cool lead. As he commented with a sarcastic giggle, 'Anybody bigger than me is going to have a really hard time. It felt like E10 but was probably E4 6a.' Afterwards Cubby remarked:

> The lead by Lynn was excellent and fearless. It brought home to me that although she says she has no interest in death-defying routes she still has an apparent lack of fear, amazing confidence and a cool head in difficult and dangerous situations. She was an inspiration and undoubtedly one of the best people I have climbed with. Although not used to the style of hard British traditional climbing with marginal gear, she adapted incredibly well. I was impressed by her focus and intelligence on the rock and her controlled sense of adventure.

Daylight was fading fast, but they wanted to reach the belay stance below the final overhang pitch before dark. Although very exposed, the wall sandwiched between the overhangs was relatively easy and full of good holds in comparison with the climbing below and they soon reached the belay. Their climbing halted by nightfall, they fixed their ropes to the belay and abseiled to the ground, leaving their ropes in place so they could ascend them the following day to attempt the last pitch.

Pabbay provided a virtually surreal background to the events taking place on the rock face. The tensions involved in attempting a first ascent of what was almost certainly one of the hardest rock routes in Britain bore little relationship to the tranquillity of the island. Lying at the southern end of a chain that stretches almost 125 miles (200 km) from Lewis in the north to Berneray in the south, it is rarely visited and arrangements have to be specially made to land here. 'Pabbay' means 'hermit's island' and it has been said that this refers to the inhabitants of the island at the time of the Norse settlement of the Hebrides in the ninth century. In fact, Pabbay is one of several hermits' islands in the Hebrides and was probably chosen for a religious retreat because of its isolation. Although separated from its nearest neighbours of Mingulay and Sandray by only 2½ and 4 miles (4 km and 6.5 km) respectively, these are not seen from the former settlement in Bàgh Bàn ('white bay') and the feeling, particularly during the sudden storms that are typical of the Outer Hebrides, is one of isolation and vulnerability.

The island is made of some of the oldest rocks in the world: layered gneiss, tilting from west to east and providing both the excellent sea-cliff climbing and the island's distinctive profile. The few visitors who come here today nearly all travel from Castlebay on Barra, where a local boatman can be hired. This can be a precarious affair and subject to the weather. Only the rasping 'crek crek' call of the corncrake, with its round-the-clock barrage of noise, disturbs the peace. It is hard to imagine this barren land sustaining a small community, and the lifestyle of its one-time inhabitants can have been barely more than a subsistence existence. There are still numerous reminders of the people who formerly dwelt here, and while the most obvious ruined building dates only from the end of the nineteenth century, it is next to a prominent mound thought to date from prehistoric times. This is said to be a graveyard, and a Pictish stone with carving can easily be found too.

Cubby and Lynn were camping in front of wooden sheep-pens and had an uninterrupted view east across the turquoise ocean which, on the clearest of days, provides a view of the mainland. But despite such idyllic surroundings, Cubby and Lynn kept their thoughts clearly focused on the rock face and set off the following day with the hope of finishing the climb.

The weather was still good, as it often is in May and June, but the cliff remained damp until the afternoon. Cubby and Lynn had got into the routine of starting late and finishing late, but with their hired boat *Mary Doune* expected at 5 p.m. the next afternoon to take them off the island so that Lynn could catch her flight back to the States, there was now a sense of urgency to get to the cliff and start working the top pitch. By midday they had climbed their ropes to their high point of the day before and were ensconced on the belay below the overhanging arch.

Cubby set off to lead the intimidating pitch, but in his heart he knew this was ambitious. As an experienced climber, he knew the boundary between on-sight climbing and hard terrain that needed inspection, working and repeated practice of the moves before it could be climbed in one push (known as redpointing). He reached the second of the stepped roofs and was stopped by a hard move with the prospect of a nasty fall if he failed. Prudently he rested on a runner. From now on he concentrated on working out each move in isolation, then later linking groups of moves together. It took him two hours to solve a particularly problematic section over the second overlap to the start of the main overhang. At first he thought it was impossible, but slowly he worked out a combination of moves which brought success. At a resting-point at the back of the ceiling, Cubby looked backwards at the awesome prospect, then took a deep breath and launched out under the ceiling. The holds were good at first and quickly he was in striking distance of the lip, but here was the hardest move of the climb. So tenuous was the climbing, using small fingerholds and contorted heel hooks, that Cubby could not link the individual moves together, repeatedly falling into space before pulling up on the rope to try a new sequence. It was early evening before Cubby managed to pull over the lip, having managed to work out the moves and link most of them together. It was a superhuman effort that left him drained physically and mentally. He lowered back down to Lynn, who had been patiently belaying for six hours. It was now Lynn's turn to try.

'I reckon the grade is 8b, perhaps 8b+,' Cubby warned Lynn, then: 'See what you think.'

The move over the second overlap proved to be impossible using Cubby's method. Lynn simply could not reach the hold. 'Sick!' she commented, on the point of giving up. But then she tried an amazing sequence slightly to the right which involved jamming her foot in the crack and using this leg as a hold or lever for her other foot while holding on to a small crystal with her thumb. It worked, and she reached the roof. On the crux moves under the overhang she fine-tuned Cubby's sequence, and again it was cunning legwork and footwork

Cubby's last-gasp redpoint attempt on the upper overhang. He is heel hooking to take some of the strain off his arms in this very strenuous position. The next few feet to the lip are the hardest on the climb.

which relieved the strain on her fingers. It was like watching a ballet being choreographed, a gymnast training and a grand master play chess, all in a crazy upside-down world.

Normally after such a hard day it requires at least a couple of days of rest before the muscles and mind have recovered sufficiently for another attempt. Unfortunately, they had no such luxury. If they were going to redpoint the climb it had to be done on the following day.

It made sense for Cubby to make the last-gasp attempt. He had managed to link all the moves together on the crux, whereas Lynn had not perfected the sequence. Conditions were far from perfect. As they were forced by the timetable to climb in the morning, the rock oozed moisture, a crucial factor that could be the difference between success and failure. 'Good luck! And give it your best!' Lynn shouted.

Surprising himself, Cubby climbed through the lower hard section of overlaps and reached the resting-point before the horizontal overhang. He stayed there for

TRAVELLING TO PABBAY

It is possible to reach Barra (the nearest inhabited island) either by air from Glasgow (British Airways) or by ferry (Caledonian MacBrayne) from either Oban or Mallaig on the mainland. All ferry services operate to a complicated timetable, so detailed planning is necessary. The ferries also convey vehicles, but advance booking is essential during most of the summer season.

Local boatmen can be hired to make the journey from Castlebay on Barra to Pabbay but these services can easily be disrupted by bad weather. An alternative for a party of six or more is to hire a boat from the mainland and use this as a base. In particular, the extended Robinson family from Doune Marine in Knoydart (tel: 01687 462667) are used to working with climbers and provide a first-class all-weather boat (the *Mary Doune*), equally good catering and excellent company. They are also very flexible, and if the weather proves unsuitable can suggest alternatives that might be more practicable.

Food and other supplies can be purchased at Castlebay.

what seemed an eternity, regaining his composure, shaking first one arm and then the other, trying to recover strength and chalking up continuously as the sweating rock greased his hands.

Cubby climbed confidently across the overhang but inadvertently hooked his leg over his arm, an acrobatic and strenuous technique called a figure of four. At the last good hold under the ceiling, he clipped the runners, chalked up and took a deep breath for the crux sequence. His performance had been perfect so far.

The initial moves of the crux sequence were the most powerful on the route and required a perfect body position. With absolute concentration he contorted his hips and then toe- and heel-hooked, enabling him to reach the crucial hold. Every muscle strained and in tension, suddenly his foot slipped and instantly he swung off, the fall held by the rope. 'It might have been the moisture, tiredness or I could have rushed it a little and not placed my foot exactly. There was no margin for error,' Cubby commented afterwards.

Cubby pulled up and regained the holds before the crux sequence and tried again. This time his foot held and he reached the lip and clipped the last runner, but his foot slipped and he fell a second time. Back on the rock again, he reached the larger holds above the lip and pulled up to the top. Lynn seconded the pitch, using aid to help remove all the gear. 'A magnificent failure,' she said, on reaching Cubby just as the boat appeared. 'It could be one of the hardest routes in Britain, even though we failed to free-climb all the top pitch. Probably worth E7 7a with the two points of aid we used. When it goes free it will be E9 7a with the top pitch 8b or 8b+.'

'I guess we could call it To Be Continued,' quipped Cubby.

A school of whales played in *Mary Doune*'s wake as she made good progress across the Sea of the Hebrides. The beer was out and the music played as Skye and Rhum filled the horizon. It started to rain, and the forecast was that bad weather would continue for a week, but they did not care. Pabbay seemed a different world from the lights of Mallaig harbour twinkling in the distance. Soon the week would be a distant memory – or would it? Cubby was already making plans to return.

The Cederberg, South Africa

6

would rather not go in. This place holds bad memories for me.' These two short sentences came as a shock. They were spoken by Ed February, one of South Africa's best rock-climbers, who minutes before had been enthusing to Joe Simpson about the wild beauty and superb climbing to be found as they travelled through the Cederberg.

For almost an hour Ed had been piloting (rather than driving) the Volkswagen Microbus as it negotiated the pot-holes and pitted ruts of the dirt road. They were on a switchback taking them to the heart of this wilderness region just three hours from Cape Town. Their hired vehicle was pulling a trailer loaded with climbing gear, provisions for a week and a generous amount of alcohol. Behind, it threw up copious amounts of fine red dust, but Ed did not seem to notice as the speedometer kept nudging 60 miles (96 km) an hour. The mood had been one of blossoming friendship as they swapped climbing stories and other reminiscences, but that had suddenly changed as the vehicle approached the farm, where it was necessary to get permission from the

High above the ground on the exposed third pitch traverse of Energy Crisis, Joe Simpson looks aghast as Ed February hangs strenuously from the sandstone edge and tries to place a cam for protection.

farmer before the pair could climb at a rock outcrop in the Cederberg known as Wolfberg. Joe Simpson listened with growing incredulity as Ed described how, only a few years before, he had been made to leave this land at gunpoint. He had not committed any crime, disobeyed any rules, or caused any danger. In fact, he had only one problem in the eyes of the landowner – he was black. Ed later summed up the experience of being a black South African in one emotional sentence: 'Why,' he half-pleaded, half-asked, 'has my whole life been linked with apartheid?'

Ed February was born in 1955 and is, by any standards, a brilliant rockclimber. He inherited a great love of the outdoors from his parents, who christened him Edmund after the New Zealander Sir Edmund Hillary. It was Hillary and Sherpa Tenzing Norgay who were the first people to stand on the summit of Everest. Appearing both impulsive and impatient, Ed is none the less a charming man whose thick, jet-black hair is now greying. At 5 foot 4 inches (1.6 m), he is not as tall as his presence suggests, and he is never seen without his glasses. 'The folks,' as Ed calls his parents, 'were into the outdoors. From a very early age we'd go hiking, and the folks loved travelling so we would explore extensively.' This is a greater achievement than anyone not born on the wrong side of South Africa's racial divide would realize. 'It was very difficult to travel if you weren't white: you weren't allowed on municipal campsites and there were very few hotels you could use.' Yet Ed's interest in the outdoors also came from another source. He was 'the smallest kid on the block' and found his poor eyesight a big handicap. 'You can't see because you haven't got specs and you haven't worked out that you can't see because you need spectacles. You can't kick any balls... You're just a useless kid. Nobody is interested in playing with the useless kid on the block, so I used to go off and do other things.' Living in the shadow of Table Mountain, which dominates the Cape Town skyline, Ed walked out of his front door and spent most of his time there. Eventually, a love of walking and cycling developed into an interest in exploring more vertical ground.

The climbers he wanted to emulate were the famous Joe Brown and Don Whillans, who were among the best of Britain's postwar climbers, but it was a white South African who played a key part in Ed's development. Ed can still picture the exact moment in 1974 when Dave Cheesmond, a leading white South African climber who was born in Durban but had moved to Cape Town, introduced himself to him, and suddenly climbing became a serious part of his life. 'I was climbing with a local lad and we met Dave Cheesmond, who said: "You guys have got potential. Why don't you come and climb with me?" No white guy would have done that. My folks didn't understand at all and said: "What is it he wants out of you?" But Dave was just being gregarious Dave and looking for a climbing partner.' This friendship was of crucial significance to Ed. He was introduced to the Cederberg; he led his first serious routes but, most important, Dave Cheesmond became a valuable catalyst. 'It was Dave who gave me the vision to realize what my potential was,' is how Ed now describes their relationship.

Today he is one of the few black climbers in South Africa, and for many years he publicly claimed to be the only one who climbed at a high standard. In a country where wage levels are comparatively low and where, until the last few years, career prospects for black people were extremely limited, Ed has managed to travel extensively. He loves the experience of being in wild, remote places and savours the freedom of moving gracefully over rock. He has climbed throughout America, most notably in Yosemite Valley but also in the Midwest and, in Ed's phrase, 'a host of other places'. Ten years ago 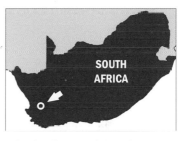 he made a couple of visits to Britain and undertook routes in Llanberis, on the grit around Stanage and on the limestone at Stoney Middleton. In the course of three trips to the Alps he succeeded on the west face of the Blaitière, the central pillar of the Frêney on Mont Blanc and the Frendo Spur on the Aiguilles du Midi, together with 'a couple of other things I forget the names of'. Within Africa Ed made an attempt to climb Mount Kenya but the weather was so atrocious that he ended up doing a lot of rock-climbing instead. He travelled to Zimbabwe to open a number of hard sport routes and believes the country potentially has some of the finest sports climbing on granite in southern Africa. In addition, the country offers a number of other fine routes that are reminiscent of the domes in Yosemite National Park's Tuolumne

▶ The Wolfberg escarpment in the Cederberg mountains. The route Energy Crisis climbs the isolated buttress with the sun catching the top in the centre of the picture.

SOUTH AFRICA'S CLIMBING HISTORY

The first recorded mountaineering exploit was an ascent of Table Mountain by Antonio de Saldanha, an admiral in the Portuguese navy, in 1503. By the time a permanent colony was established at the Cape by the Dutch in 1652 it was common practice for sailors, whose ships stopped here on the way to India, to climb Table Mountain. Rock-climbing started in South Africa in 1885 with a dramatic solo ascent of the rock tower called Toverkop in Cape Province by Gustav Nefdt, a 19-year-old local boy with no climbing experience.

Climbing popularity grew at the end of the nineteenth century and the Mountain Club of South Africa was formed in 1891. By the end of the last century there were 50 different routes up Table Mountain, with George Travers-Jackson being the most influential climber of the day. Climbing spread through South Africa, and in 1920 a milestone was reached when George Londt climbed a difficult route up the front face of Klein Winterhoek. Also active at this time were Cobern, Fraser, Cameron (who opened up the Cederberg) and Berrisford (who made over 120 first ascents).

In 1931 the Cape Province Mountain Club was formed by climbers of mixed race unable to join the Mountain Club due to racial segregation.

The period immediately after the Second World War brought a revolution in equipment and standards, and in the 1960s Rusty Baillie (who came from Rhodesia) pioneered many hard free and aid climbs. The 1970s and 1980s saw a new breed of young rock-climbers, in particular Dave Cheesmond, Tony Dick, Ed February, Dave Davies, Chris Lomax, Kevin Smith, Greg Lacey and Andy de Klerk, who pushed up the standards to equal those in Europe and North America. Not only did they make an impact in their own country, but they made significant ascents throughout the world.

The last five years have seen an explosive growth in sport climbing, and the reputation of the quality of the climbing in South Africa has been confirmed by many visiting climbers such as Todd Skinner (USA) and Fredric Nicole (Switzerland).

Meadows. Other trips have included visits to Malawi, Namibia and Lesotho and currently he has plans to make a first visit to Mali. It is a measure of Ed's commitment to climbing that he has also been to Thailand, Nepal, Malaysia and Borneo.

The problem with climbing out of South Africa is that the rand isn't worth much on the international exchange and we don't get paid very well either, and as a result funding many of these trips oneself isn't very easy. The early trips to France were sponsored by my university – they have a travel grant which students can apply to, and I managed to get that on a sporting bursary so I was lucky. Many of the other trips were just saving.

Within South Africa's western Cape Province, Ed has climbed most of the traditional-style routes, adding that selecting two or three special routes 'would just be picking out memories of having a great day out with some great friends'. Two of those special routes are on Krakadouw, north of the Cederberg, and fit firmly into that category. Ichthiosaurus, which Ed made the first ascent of with Andy de Klerk and Tienie Versfeld, is 'a fine line up a beautiful wall and we just had a complete laugh the whole day. The crux pitch was 22/23 and I was pulling through it with absolute pure control. I was just flowing, it was great. It is still a very special route to me. The other route is called Australopthicus: it was opened by me and Tienie and I believe it's the hardest multi-pitch route in the Cederberg area. It's just this beautiful, dead-straight line going up these corners and grooves at a consistent grade above 20 for 9 pitches. The easiest pitch is 20; the hardest pitch is 24. It took us two days but it was a great route.'

Since 1990 Ed February has worked as an archaeologist and palaeoenvironmentalist at the South African Museum at Cape Town, where he specializes in the identification of wood and charcoal from archaeological sites and is presently conducting research into providing a better understanding of climate change in his country. In the old South Africa it was a struggle to develop a career and often Ed had to battle his way into a job, overturning a number of preconceptions about his

▶ There are a number of excellent bolted sport routes on the beautiful sandstone towers of Kromriver in the Cederberg, which provided Ed and Joe with ideal warm-up climbs before they attempted Energy Crisis.

ability on the way. He has also succeeded in balancing his professional work with a commitment to climbing. Only in the last three years has he joined the Mountain Club of South Africa after more than two decades of animosity between him and the club. As a young climber he had been affronted when members of what used to be a whites-only club taunted him when he was on a route; he agreed to join the club only when its constitution was amended so as to include a clause specifically committing the club to an anti-racist stance. Now Ed is somewhat bemused to find himself on the committee, adding: 'Everything works both ways: because of their attitude to me, I developed a weird attitude to them. It was them and us. We've just had a huge history of fighting which I hope we have come to an amicable agreement on.'

Although he had not previously met Joe Simpson, like virtually all climbers he knew of Joe from the epic tale of survival told in *Touching the Void*. Joe, who is now 37, is 5 foot, 9 inches (1.75 m) tall but is squat and powerful in appearance and has a right arm that seems as if it has been fashioned for drinking. A scarred nose is only the most obvious sign of his past injuries. For a long time he walked with a pronounced limp, following accidents on Pachermo and most famously on Siula Grande in the Peruvian alps, where he engaged in a battle for survival as heroic as any undertaken in this century. In June 1985 disaster struck shortly after Joe and his partner Simon Yates left the summit of this 21,000-foot (6400-m) mountain. They had attempted this new route as a lightweight expedition comprising just the pair of them, knowing that if they had any accident only their own efforts could save them and that there would be no possibility of outside help and rescue. When Joe slipped and broke his leg, Simon struggled to get him down the mountain by lowering him on their climbing-rope, but during one of these manoeuvres in the dark the rope caught and stuck solid. When Simon began to be pulled off his makeshift belay the situation became desperate, and he had no option but to take an agonizing decision and cut the rope that was holding Joe. It was only three days later when Joe crawled into base camp semi-conscious, badly dehydrated and in agony from his multiple injuries, that Simon realized that his actions had not killed Joe but helped to save his life.

Joe's hour-by-hour account of his battle for survival is chillingly told in *Touching the Void*, which has since become an international best-seller and established Joe as a sensitive and perceptive writer. Yet the widespread recognition that came with his written account has also had its downside. Joe is an incredibly talented, bold climber who is now mainly known to the public at large as the result of an accident rather than for his climbing achievements. He is a complex individual who is always deprecating his standard of climbing and who talks constantly to hide any insecurity. He is argumentative in a pleasant way and can be relied on to have an opinion on absolutely everything. His upbringing in a service family that was regularly on the move, and his education at the well-known Catholic public school Ampleforth, where 20 priests assembled for Mass every Sunday, have undoubtedly left their mark. Today, Joe views himself as a writer, but while the four books that followed *Touching the Void* demonstrate a writer of wide range and talent, he is still an adventurous climber in spite of his injuries.

Although he would describe himself as a mountaineer rather than a rock-climber, he has climbed throughout Britain on all types of rock. He is an accomplished alpinist with a wealth of experience in both winter and summer and has undertaken many of the classic hard routes on north faces, such as the Walker Spur on the Grandes Jorasses. Joe's record on expeditions is no less impressive: he has undertaken trips to Pakistan, Tibet, Nepal, Ecuador and Peru. In reciting this list Joe finally lost patience with himself and concluded in a typically combative way: 'I've never been asked to do this before but I've done quite a bit! Most of this is since I've broken my leg and the doctor said I'd never climb again. It shows how wrong they are.'

These expeditions have been distinguished by either the style in which they have been undertaken or by the routes that were chosen.

I'd far rather climb the north spur of Ranrapalca than climb Cho Oyu. I'd much sooner do an alpine-style ascent of a fine aesthetic hard route than go and climb a 25,250-foot (8000-m) peak that's climbed by everyone simply because of its height. The British climbers I admire are people like Mick Fowler, the late Brendan Murphy and Andy Cave, who are going out, climbing at the highest standard, putting it all together and doing incredible routes.

When Joe was asked to name his favourite route he answered in a typically perverse way by choosing one that he had not actually climbed. At the age of 12 he read *The White Spider*, Heinrich Harrer's classic account of the first ascent of the Eiger's notorious north face just prior to the outbreak of the Second World War and recalls that 'it scared the shit out of me'. Joe was impressed by many aspects of that first ascent including its historical context, the difficulties posed by the route and by the style in which it was climbed. Years later, Joe became obsessed with the idea of climbing north faces and had succeeded on many of them but had never attempted the Eiger. In fact he was in hospital in Sheffield when his partner on Siula Grande, Simon Yates, went off and climbed it. 'I was bloody pissed off about that!' Joe exclaimed, adding, 'It is a seminal climb that I haven't done and, although I could do it now, I don't think I ever will.' Joe's reasoning is simple: once he has completed a climb it changes from being a dream to becoming reality, and to illustrate the point Joe recalls sitting on top of the Walker Spur on his twenty-first birthday. 'I'd wanted to do the Walker for years and I couldn't imagine climbing it. When I did, I ruined the dream.' Yet despite his appalling accident he still counts his ascent of Siula Grande as one of his most important. As he explained:

> I was obsessed with a new route. I had never done a first ascent and it was my first. It was a very good climb and it got completely overshadowed by what happened – understandably – which was a shame. It has never been repeated, probably because people have been put off by the descent. Basically, we just screwed up really.

Joe also has a number of unusual ascents to his credit. These include direct lines on Nelson's Column in Trafalgar Square, and routes on the Houses of Parliament, Harrods and Australia House, together with less-distinguished monuments like industrial chimneys. He has justified these climbs, which he undertook, along with John Stevenson, as Greenpeace 'actions', saying: 'I make no apology…for saying that our Greenpeace actions are the most worthwhile things we have ever done.' Joe admits that at first he 'prostituted' himself 'not to the environmental movement but to the adrenalin surge of fear and exhilaration that comes with these actions. Our approach was soon tempered by the terrible facts revealed to us by

▶ Ed seconds the first pitch of Energy Crisis belayed by Joe above. He is bridged across the corner, conserving his strength, before he starts the strenuous layback.

Greenpeace campaigners.' In the course of campaigning on a variety of issues, from saving whales, fur-bearing animals and the ozone layer, and trying to stop atom-bomb testing, Joe was arrested countless times, acquired a criminal record and, on occasion, assaulted, but he is pleased that 'for once in our lives we set aside our selfish ambitions, took the high moral ground and protested to the world with right on our side'.

After only a day together it was obvious that, despite coming from totally different backgrounds, Joe and Ed had many things in common, of which climbing and having a good time came pretty near the top of their list. Prior to their meeting, Joe had been apprehensive about forming a natural relationship with Ed, yet within minutes any fears were dispelled. Ed was delighted to be partnering Joe but was concerned that he should see the new South Africa in a positive light. The Cederberg region is one of great personal importance to him, so he was delighted when Joe obviously shared his enthusiasm for it. After the eventual collecting of their permit, the Microbus completed its final few miles down the dirt road to Kromriver Farm, where the pair had rented

WEATHER AND VEGETATION

The Cape has a semi-arid Mediterranean climate but the Cederberg is more extreme. Winter, between May and September, can be cold and wet, and it often snows in the higher parts and night-time temperatures drop sharply. In the summer temperatures often reach as high as 40˚C. In general the best time to climb is in the spring (mid-September and October) or autumn (April to mid-May).

The vegetation is predominantly mountain *Fynbos* (fine bush) and is defined by the presence of white-flowering protea bushes and numerous species of heather, grass and sedges. There are few tree species apart from the rare Clanwilliam cedar, after which the region is named. The geology of the area is one of bedded sandstone.

a cottage for the following week. With just an hour or so to sunset, the vehicle and its trailer were unpacked, cans of beer tentatively opened to see that they had survived the buffeting (a vital safety procedure Joe may well have learnt from Aid Burgess), and climbing gear quickly checked to ensure that nothing vital had got left behind. Joe, sensing a quick opportunity to indulge his other great passion, grabbed his fishing-rod and tried a few abortive casts before the sun finally disappeared behind one of the many small peaks and the opportunity for another beer seemed a more sensible option. Tonight was a chance to relax, swap stories and sink a few cans before the hard work began.

In the morning Joe felt jaded from the travel.

'How about a warm-up climb? I need to familiarize myself with the rock down here,' he suggested. Ed agreed and they spent the day at a beautiful area of pinnacles nearby, where there were a number of bolted sport climbs.

Next day it was a short drive on dusty gravel roads from Kromriver Farm to the parking in the valley bottom. High above, the Wolfberg escarpment of red and ochre rock stood like a medieval castle wall protecting the high plateau behind. Ed pointed out a 330-foot- (100-m)-high buttress standing majestically and slightly separate from the main cliffs.

'The route, Energy Crisis, goes straight up the middle of the buttress and finishes on the prominent prow at the top.'

'Looks spectacular. How hard is it?' Joe quizzed, already wondering whether he could keep up with Ed.

'Don't worry. It's only grade 20, lad,' Ed replied, then added: 'That's South Africa grade, but I guess it would be E2 in the UK.'

'Hard enough for a mountaineer like me,' Joe replied, already making excuses for his fitness.

Although it was mid-September – early spring in the Cederberg – the morning sky was clear and the temperature was rising. The climb was south-facing and luckily would remain in the shade all day, but the three-quarter-hour walk up the steep hillside would be hot work so Joe and Ed wore only T-shirts and shorts.

They started up the track through the semi-arid landscape brought to life by the winter rains. Eye-catching yellow daisies mixed with pink, white and purple heathers were in profusion, and higher, as the path snaked through huge boulders

and between small cliffs, large protea bushes dominated the vegetation. Ed and Joe were not alone. Groups of walkers shared their path, heading for The Cracks and The Arch, two famous geological features near the Wolfberg cliff. It was noticeable that all the hikers were white and it was obvious that there had not been much of a shift in the recreation habits in the new rainbow nation of South Africa.

As they walked, Joe asked whether the climbing on Energy Crisis would be similar to the bolted sport routes on the cliffs near Kromriver, which they had climbed the day before as a warm-up. 'The rock is the same but we follow cracks and all the protection is natural; either nuts or cams,' Ed replied. Joe asked if Ed was against bolts. 'No, lad. I just climb rock. But my main love is traditional, naturally protected adventure climbing in the mountains, and I regard bolted sport climbs more as training.'

Ed then explained some of the problems that South African climbers are having with access and bolting.

Access to climb is a big problem in South Africa, and usually we have to ask for a permit to climb on a cliff. On private land we have to negotiate rights to climb, and in places like Montagu the landowners are happy for us to climb and use bolts. This has encouraged a lot of younger climbers to go there as they tend to prefer athletic sport climbs protected by bolts.

But it is a balance, and in areas such as here in Cederberg there is a very delicate situation. It is run by the Cape Nature Conservation, who are now wanting to impose a recreation management plan on the wilderness area. They don't want bolts on cliffs like Wolfberg, but maybe they will allow some areas to be bolted, like Kromriver or Rocklands. In fact, there are already quite a few bolted climbs in these two areas, and they have turned a blind eye to the existing routes but have made it plain that future indiscriminate bolting will not be tolerated. Anything that disturbs the status quo could be disastrous for climbing. It's like the situation in many of the national parks in the United States and in some areas of the UK.

◄ Ed starts the uncompromising layback. This is the only method to climb the wide corner crack, due to the holdless sandstone, on the first pitch of Energy Crisis.

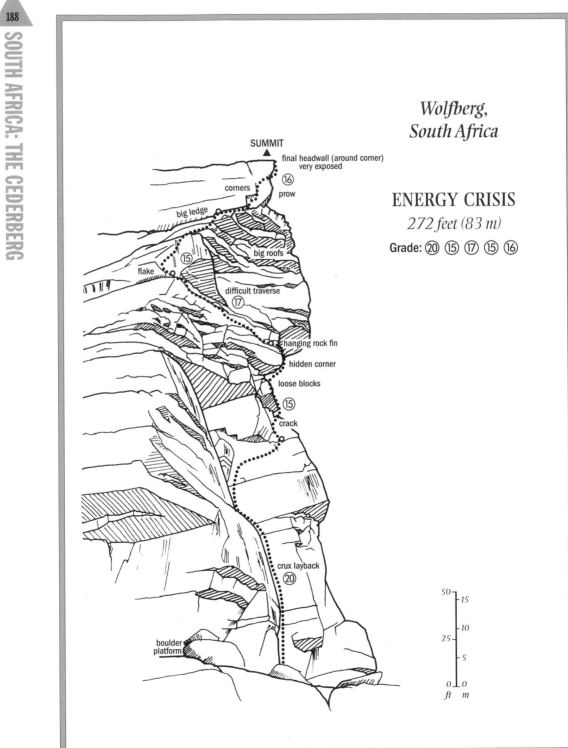

Wolfberg,
South Africa

ENERGY CRISIS
272 feet (83 m)

Grade: ⑳ ⑮ ⑰ ⑮ ⑯

SUMMIT

final headwall (around corner)
very exposed

⑯

corners   prow

big ledge

⑮   big roofs

flake

difficult traverse

⑰

hanging rock fin

hidden corner

loose blocks

⑮

crack

crux layback

⑳

boulder
platform

50 — 15

— 10

25 —
— 5

0 — 0
ft   m

Ed then illustrated the problem with a story he had heard the day before.

It made me so angry when Olive [owner of Kromriver Farm] told me about the young student climber who upset her by driving fast through her land and then went climbing at Kromriver without a permit. I can understand why she called the police, but what it did was draw the attention of the Cape Nature Conservation to the need for a management plan. But all they will see is that if climbers can't behave sensibly, what hope is there of them adhering to a management plan. It not only threatens the use of bolts it threatens our freedom to climb. And now it is my job as official rock-climbing representative of the Cape Town section of the General Committee of the Mountain Club of South Africa to sort it all out!

As they neared the base Ed showed Joe the line followed by Energy Crisis. When it was first climbed by Barley and Smithers in 1979 it must have been very difficult to envisage a route, as the whole buttress bristled with triangular overhanging slabs of sandstone. The only weakness was a groove near the centre; this opened into a corner which slanted right to the edge of the buttress to an impasse of large overhangs. The route cleverly avoided these by traversing horizontally to the left then weaving its way through more overhangs before attacking the final prow that jutted from the centre of the cliff.

At the bottom they unpacked their rucksacks and decided who would lead the various parts of the climb. The route was described as 272 feet (83 m) long and divided into five pitches. Joe volunteered to lead the first two, leaving Ed with the top three.

Immediately, Joe regretted choosing the first pitch as the initial moves were far harder than he expected. From the ground the groove looked quite benign, but the first decent hold was at head height and the left wall did not have the normal good friction of the Cape sandstone. Because of his many accidents, Joe's ankles and knees had been seriously weakened and even a fall from a few feet above the ground would have had serious consequences and brought the climb to a premature end. 'Go for it. You can do it, lad!' encouraged Ed in his South African accent liberally laced with Americanisms.

'I'm worried about my left foot zipping off. God I worry about everything,' Joe replied in his typical self-critical way. Then, as he struggled: 'Damn. I'm pumped. It's strange how quickly you get pumped when you haven't warmed up.' Joe forced his right leg on to a good hold and stood up. 'Lovely jubbly, jam city,' he said as he reached good holds and jams in the crack above then placed a good nut runner to protect him from the potential ground fall.

'Hang a London bus off that runner! I feel happier now,' he shouted to Ed. Ten feet (3 metres) higher, the groove was capped by a small overhang and above opened into an 'open book' corner, holdless apart from a wide crack where the two side walls met. This section had the reputation of being one of the hardest parts of the climb.

Joe climbed to below the overhang and bridged his feet on the corner side walls, taking most of the strain from his arms. He then placed a large cam for protection in the wide crack above, clipped his rope in and started to work out how to make progress. It was obvious that the only way to climb the crack was by layback, a strenuous and difficult technique where the hands hold the side of the crack and the legs are brought up to chest height and pressed on the opposite side wall of the crack. But to start the layback required a committing and difficult move and, once started, offered no possibility of retreat, rest or stops to place protection until a good ledge 16 feet (5 m) higher.

As when standing on a high diving board, Joe's mind was in turmoil – an inner schizophrenic debate where the sensible and logical instinct was to say no and retreat, but to succeed he had to overcome these doubts and trust his strength and skill. Tentatively, he reached high with his hands and placed his right foot on a hold. It did not feel right. After some time Ed shouted impatiently: 'You must get your right leg higher.' Joe followed Ed's advice and this position seemed more hopeful.

'Blind as well as stupid,' Joe answered in the banter that was becoming a feature of their relationship.

'OK, lad, layback and think of England,' encouraged Ed.

With hands pulling and legs pushing, Joe brought his legs up high and walked

Joe climbs the hanging fin of rock. A few feet higher, however, he got stuck as he tried to reach the second belay on an exposed ledge up and left just out of sight.

them up the wall. 'Scary – seriously worrying bloody thing. What a way to start the day!' Joe stuttered. The ledge above seemed a mile away and Joe was out of breath and rapidly running out of power. Just as his strength gave out, he grabbed the ledge. Unfortunately, Joe had tangled his rope: not an immediate problem, but higher it could jam and cause serious inconvenience.

'You've crossed your ropes,' alerted Ed.

'I couldn't give a flying fuck!' Joe shouted, thankful just to get to the top.

'Good one, lad! The style of a bloody gazelle!' congratulated Ed.

'An octopus on acid,' was Joe's retort. 'I wish I hadn't given up cigarettes. I need one now,' he added. Joe stood on the small ledge for some time, calming his nerves and resting his tired arms.

'What you doing up there, Simpson?' impatiently shouted the hyperactive Ed in a good-humoured way.

As Joe climbed the easier crack and corner above, he started to enjoy himself and the layback became a fading nightmare. 'I'm just going to do the traverse to the belay ledge, Ed. It looks pretty easy.'

'Cool,' Ed shouted.

Joe placed a couple of nuts in the crack above and tied the rope to them. When he was secure he took in the remaining rope, made more difficult by the tangle he had created in the panic to complete the layback.

'OK, lad, that's me, ready when you are,' Ed yelled.

'OK – enjoy,' replied Joe in a false American accent.

Ed was on his home turf, climbing on this type of sandstone since childhood and, with the security from the rope above, he flowed up the pitch, making light work of the layback. His experience and skill as a top rock athlete, performing well within himself, contrasted with Joe's more frantic efforts near his climbing limit. 'Why are you not breathing like a broken-down steam engine?' Joe asked. Ed just laughed.

Joe soon started up the second pitch. Good holds and rough rock were a joy to climb but after 33 feet (10 m) Joe pulled round an arête, out of sight of Ed, on to some large loose blocks. Carefully, he distributed his weight, conscious of not putting too much pressure on any one hold, and cautiously reached a ledge. Where the hell do I go now, thought Joe. Above, the rock jutted out in a series of dramatic overhangs formed by the strata of the different layers of sandstone. To the right the rock was dangerously rotten. The guidebook had described the route moving left, but this looked very difficult as the only weakness was a hanging fin of rock protruding out from the overhangs above. Joe could not see what was at the top of the fin but prayed that there was a ledge and easier ground around the corner.

On closer inspection the fin was covered in good holds. The mix of relatively simple climbing with dramatic exposure as he moved up and left with only space below his feet was a joy – a feeling shared by most climbers when in control and on easy ground but as soon as difficulties are encountered and with them the possibility of a fall, then our natural fear of height comes to the fore and the exposure can be terrifying.

A wide horizontal crack was formed where the fin met the overhangs, and Joe soon hung on the good holds below the crack and peered hopefully around the corner. With relief he saw a good ledge just above and to the left. Unfortunately, in his impatience to pull on to the ledge he made a complete hash of the moves. Rather than keeping low and swinging dramatically around on to the ledge, he wriggled into the false security of the crack and managed to wedge his now horizontal body. He could touch the ledge with his hands, but when he tried to pull on to it the gear attached to his harness jammed in the crack. 'What the bloody 'ell are you doing, Simpson?' laughed Ed, at the amusing sight of Joe's legs sticking out horizontally from the rock high above.

'I'm stuck,' came the muffled reply followed by a string of expletives.

Because he thought that reaching the ledge would be relatively straightforward, Joe had not put in much protection and his last runner was some way below. Faced with a potentially long fall and unable to unclip any gear from his harness for further protection, Joe did not see the amusing side of his predicament. With a lot of pulling and pushing and more effort than should have been necessary, he slowly and precariously squirmed on his stomach out of the crack and arrived on the ledge in a rather dishevelled manner. 'I'm at the belay ledge!' shouted an exhausted

▶ Ed leads across the exposed traverse on the third pitch of Energy Crisis (the same position as in the picture on page 170). Ed will traverse a further 20 feet (6 m) to the left and belay. The climb then avoids the overhangs by climbing up the darker rock full of holds.

Joe. Ed followed the pitch but, forewarned about the difficulties, reached Joe's spectacular perch by using some large hidden holds above the horizontal crack.

With overhanging rock above and below, the position was very exposed. Although anchored securely to the rock, there is always doubt and insecurity when in such a position. The feeling was exacerbated by the hillside below, which dropped steeply to the wide valley.

'You get the feeling that if there was an earthquake the whole lot would fall down,' Joe joked, then hopefully and with a sudden change of tone asked Ed: 'This isn't an earthquake zone, is it?'

'Yes. There was quite a big one in 1969 which brought down a lot of rock,' replied Ed with a wry smile.

'Oh, my God, that's the last thing I want to hear!' replied Joe.

With a little urgency they sorted out their equipment for the next pitch, which traversed left through the overhangs and was the second crux of the climb.

Ed shuffled leftwards from the belay until the ledge stopped abruptly and there was nothing but space and an awesome, gut-wrenching drop to the base of the cliff 165 feet (50 m) below. With nothing for his feet the next moves were obviously going to be both difficult and strenuous. With safety a priority, he quickly fixed protection in the horizontal crack just in reach above his head. These cracks, or rails as South African climbers call them, are a common feature of climbing in the Cape and are formed between two sandstone bedding planes. With the rope clipped into the protection, Ed started the difficult section. Joe belayed and watched in admiration as Ed climbed fast and fluidly, first by pulling up and then 'railing' left.

'Looking good!' shouted Joe.

'Yeah, it's such a cool pitch. I keep telling myself I'm on a boulder just above the ground and I don't get as scared,' Ed replied, hanging in space from just his fingers. He then carefully placed another cam for protection and continued left.

'Now for the undignified bit.' Ed had reached a point where the edge of the rail became rounded but the sandstone strata opened in a horizontal, body-width slot above. Gymnastically, he placed his toe end on a tiny hold at waist height and pulled up, pivoting his weight on to the diminutive foothold, and threw his upper body into the slot. He was now in an uncomfortable bunched-up position, but with a quick twist of the body he gained a horizontal lying position. An ungainly crawl, sandwiched between two layers of sandstone, completed the difficulties, and soon Ed was able to stand up on to a ledge on the left edge of the buttress and belay. 'OK, lad, I'm safe,' Ed yelled.

Traverses are almost as difficult for the second climber as they are for the lead climber because there is no security from a rope above. This was now all too apparent to Joe as he started to climb, looking at the rope looping horizontally towards Ed, who was belayed securely on the other side of the abyss. Joe froze, his mind flashing a warning of the horrendous fall and swing that would result from failure.

'Are you going to climb?' Ed shouted mischievously.

'No. I'm standing here trying to get my act together,' replied Joe, breathing deeply and trying to calm his adrenalin-stimulated nerves. He then tentatively moved left. 'Jesus, what a drop!' he cried and quickly retreated. Ed laughed like a hyena. 'I'll have another go in a minute, Ed,' Joe muttered nervously. This time prepared for the exposure, he took the runner out and pulled up and railed left in a manic rush, effective but lacking Ed's finesse and composure. In a blur of pulling arms and flailing legs Joe launched himself into the horizontal slot. 'Thank God for that,' exclaimed a grateful Joe as he joined Ed on the stance.

Above them the rock changed character from the monolithic slabs of ochre and pink which made up the bottom half of the buttress to deep-red rock streaked black and bright yellow by lichen. Not only did the colour change, but the smoothness was replaced by pockets, filigrees, amazing honeycombs, contorted spikes and sculpted cracks. The character of the rock reminded Joe of a vertical version of the clints and grikes found in limestone topography.

With such a featured rock there was an abundance of holds for both feet and hands and Ed speedily climbed a flake of rock above the belay, testing each hold to confirm its security. Soon he disappeared from view, but the steady movement of the rope indicated that he was finding little difficulty with the pitch. Soon the rope stopped moving and there was a shout that echoed off the surrounding cliffs like a British Rail announcement. 'What d' you say?' Joe shouted.

'I'm at the big ledge. Start climbing when you're ready,' Ed repeated, and Joe now understood.

'One more pitch and it's beer time,' Joe remarked as he reached Ed on the ledge, then, looking around, added: 'Where do we go from here?'

The route moved right and climbed a final prow of rock to the sunlit top of the cliff. Ed gained access to the prow by climbing a pleasant corner then moving right to a second, more difficult corner. A cairn of stones at its base was evidence that other climbers had avoided the first difficult pull. Ed resisted the temptation to stand on the rocks and made a tricky move to gain better holds part-way up the corner. Higher, the hold ran out and Ed moved further right on to the other side of the prow. 'Wow! Fantastic! This is spectacular!' Ed shouted as he contemplated the 300-foot (90-m) void he was now hanging above. A short, steep wall separated Ed from success, a wall that looked very arduous from below and, as if the exposure and difficulty were not enough, Ed was having trouble finding decent runners to protect the top wall. Eventually, he positioned a small wire nut in a thin crack and hoped it would hold if he fell. Carefully, he balanced up, feeling the rock for suitable holds. Where there looked to be nothing, Ed's fingers curled around hidden holds, and, pulling up, he reached a better crack and placed a good nut runner. 'Hang your mother off that one!' he shouted. Relieved to get solid protection, he reached up and again found hidden holds, but barely big enough to make the moves possible. The route had veiled its last moves carefully, and discovering the exact sequence of holds epitomized the joy of climbing to Ed. 'Wow! Fantastic!' he whooped as he pulled over the top. 'Spacey – what a great climb!' was Joe's verdict when he had followed the pitch and joined Ed at the top.

I n the few days they had together, a close friendship had developed between the two men, but as they headed back in the Microbus to Cape Town one thing was still troubling Joe. It was obvious that Ed, like all black South Africans, had suffered deeply during the years of apartheid and that suffering had affected all aspects of his life. Every night Ed and Joe had walked up to the farmhouse at Kromriver to be served an enormous meal by Olive Nieuwoudt. It would be an unremarkable scene almost anywhere in the world except South Africa. On the first evening Ed took a sharp intake of breath and quietly said to Joe: 'I just

With over 300 feet (90 m) of space below him, Joe enjoys the final moves of the climb.

don't believe this. I never thought I would be allowed into Olive Nieuwoudt's house, and here she is serving me dinner. Man, you can't understand what this means to me.' On another occasion Ed recalled Dave Cheesmond 'throwing a complete and absolute tantrum' in an office because an official refused to issue a permit for Dave and Ed to climb together. Most movingly, Ed spoke passionately about his own experience within a country divided by apartheid.

That whole apartheid legacy has left quite a big scar on me. I'm really bitter about it. I really am bitter, which is not really understandable when you actually look at the present government where many of the top people have spent years in prison. They have suffered *considerably* more than I have. Yet they come out and say we should have no retribution and that we shouldn't put our perpetrators in jail.

ED FEBRUARY AND THE SOUTH AFRICAN EVEREST EXPEDITION

In 1996 Ed February was invited to join South Africa's first Everest expedition, which had a multiracial make-up and was designed to be emblematic of the new rainbow nation. Nelson Mandela agreed to be the patron, and the enterprise, sponsored by the Johannesburg *Sunday Times*, achieved enormous publicity. Ed had harboured a dream of climbing Everest since he was a child and saw the expedition as a potent symbol of a nation trying to unify itself. Sadly, the expedition turned sour almost before it set foot on the mountain when the three leading climbers – Ed February, Andy de Klerk and Andy Hackland – found the behaviour of their leader Ian Woodall intolerable and resigned from the expedition. Woodall and another member of the team, Cathy O'Dowd, reached the summit, but Ed, de Klerk and Hackland had felt they couldn't put their lives in the hands of someone in whom they had no trust. Although Woodall is largely discredited in mountaineering circles, Ed described leaving the expedition as 'the hardest decision of my life', and on his return to South Africa found it difficult to come to terms with Woodall's behaviour. He had looked forward to the Everest trip enormously, particularly as he would not be able to finance such a major expedition himself.

Ed has enormous respect for the Mandela government and its policies but believes that it will take at least a generation to improve the lives of the majority of people and accomplish real change. Thinking back to what he terms 'the yoke of apartheid placed around my neck', Ed has one last thought on the present situation. 'We should forgive them, is what our President says. I have a lot of respect for that, I really have.' For an outsider like Joe it is harder to understand Ed's viewpoint: 'They screw up your whole life,' Joe says, 'and now you just forgive them. I just can't get my head around this Truth and Reconciliation Commission.'

But Ed's final comment is not about a political system that had dominated his life but about climbing.

Just being on this route with Joe is a great experience. I don't care about the difficulty of the rock, and I suppose that will mean I'll never be a really hard climber. Mostly I'm just not interested in training up hard enough, and you lose something when that's all you're going for – the grade. I believe you lose quite a lot. I think one has to focus on just understanding the environment and understanding the people you're with.

Sign of the times as Olive Nieuwoudt serves Ed dinner in her farmhouse at Kromriver.

CLIMBING GRADES

The level of difficulty encountered on a climb is indicated by a grade. This gives an estimation of the technical difficulties and strenuosity involved in a climb, and in some grading systems how dangerous the route is. A climber knows the maximum level to which he or she can climb, so the grade gives an idea to all those who want to repeat the climb whether they are capable of success. The climbers who make the first ascent of a climb, grade (and name) their route, though often the grade is not confirmed until the route has been repeated several times.

Different systems have evolved in different countries, but usually the basic information is conveyed by a numerical grade. The British system is unfortunately very confusing and often combines an adjectival grade, which estimates the overall difficulty of the undertaking and effort, with a numerical grade indicating the technical difficulty of the hardest moves. Even more perplexing, the adjectival grades are more often abbreviated and subdivided. For example Hard Very Severe is shortened to HVS and Extremely Severe (the hardest grade) is given the letter E and then subdivided, ranging in difficulty from E1 to E9. The technical grade is marginally easier to understand and is given a number which is subdivided into a, b or c. For no apparent reason the grade starts at 4a and the upper end of the scale is open-ended, with the hardest climb currently achieved being a hefty 7b.

To add to the bewilderment, the American system uses various classes with hiking at grade 1 and roped climbing at grade 5. This is then subdivided in an open-ended system from 5.0 to 5.14 with subdivisions of a, b, c and d with added + and - for fine tuning! The other important grade is the French one which is often used on sport climbs throughout the world. This starts at 1 and goes up to 9, being subdivided a, b and c. The more logical Australian and South African systems start at 1 and at present go up to 33. There are also German, alpine and UIAA (Union Internationale des Associations d'Alpinisme) grades to contend with! The comparison chart will help to compare the different world grading systems.

A typical grade for the same hard climb would be E5 6b in the UK, 7b in France, 26 in South Africa and 5.12b in the USA.

Snow- and ice-climbs are graded in Roman numerals, for example I is a simple snow-climb and VI would be a technically demanding ice-climb. Finally, climbs using artificial aid are given a separate grade from AO, which is simple climbing, to A5, which involves very dangerous and precarious aid climbing.

BRITAIN	USA	SOUTH AFRICA/ AUSTRALIA	FRANCE
4a	5.5		4
4b	5.6	13	
	5.7	14	5
4c		15	
5a	5.8	16	5+
	5.9	17	
5b	5.10a	18	6a
	5.10b	19	6a+
5c	5.10c	20	6b
	5.10d	21	6b+
6a	5.11a	22	6c
	5.11b	23	6c+
	5.11c	24	7a
	5.11d	25	7a+
6b	5.12a		7b
	5.12b	26	7b+
	5.12c		7c
6c	5.12d	27	
	5.13a	28	7c+
		29	8a
7a	5.13b	30	8a+
	5.13c	31	8b
	5.13d	32	8b+
7b	5.14a	33	8c

A comparative chart showing the main free-climbing grades.

Adventure Climbing *See* Traditional Climb

Aid and Aid Climbing *See* Artificial Climbing

Anchor A point of attachment on the cliff. It can be natural, such as a flake or thread, or artificial, such as a nut, cam, peg or bolt. An anchor can provide a runner or the point of attachment at a belay

Artificial Climbing Climbing which relies on anchors or aids, such as pegs, nuts, cams and bolts, for progress rather than for protection. The anchors placed in the rock or ice are used to clip in slings and etriers, which are then used as handholds and footholds. Artificial climbing generally is confined to rock which is too steep or holdless to be free-climbed

Ascender A mechanical device used to help climb a rope. Ascenders' special cams allow them to slide easily up the rope but, when weighted, they lock, preventing them from sliding down. One is attached to the waist harness, the other via a long sling to a foot loop. By alternately straightening the legs and then hanging from the waist, slow but steady progress is made up the rope

Bandoleer A shoulder sling used to carry equipment

Belay The anchoring securely to the rock face of a climber who also holds the rope by passing it through a belay device. The rope then protects the other climber in case of a fall

Belay Device A small metal plate with a hole in the centre or a tube through which the rope is passed. This bight of rope is then clipped by a karabiner on to the belayer's harness. The rope is held effortlessly during a fall by the friction of the rope as it passes through the plate in a sharp S-shape

Bolt Metal expansion bolts are placed in pre-drilled holes in the rock to make anchors. The climber, rather than the rock, determines their location, and in many areas their use is controversial as they permanently damage the rock

Bomber As in bomber gear: a very solid or secure runner or anchor

Break A horizontal crack or depression usually formed between two layers of rock strata. Good holds or a resting position are often found in a break

Bridging A climbing technique in which the feet are spread outwards and press in opposite directions. It is often used to climb two opposite walls, as found in chimneys, grooves or corners

Cam and Camming Device An anchor made of metal which expands to lodge securely in a crack. Cams come in different sizes to accommodate different widths of cracks

Chimney A wide fissure in rock into which most or all the body can fit

Corner Where two walls meet to form an approximate right-angle like an open book

Desperate Term for very difficult climbing!

Draw Also called a quick draw. A short tape sling with a karabiner at either end. The karabiners are clipped into the anchor at one end and the rope at the other to provide an extension so the rope can run freely

Etrier A short ladder, usually with three rungs, made of nylon tape. It is used to stand in when artificial climbing

Flake A thin slab of rock, which can be either huge or tiny, partially detached from the main face. When secure, flakes often provide excellent holds or, if a sling is draped over the top of them, can be used as anchors

Free-climbing Climbing using only natural holds on the rock. Rope and anchors are used to protect the climber but not to aid progress

Friend The most common make of camming device

Gear *See* Runner

Harness A special climbing harness made from wide nylon tape which is buckled around the waist and thighs. The rope is tied into the harness, and during a fall the climber's weight is distributed safely. Climbing equipment, such as karabiners, nuts and cams, are clipped on to side loops on the harness for convenient access when needed on the climb. Gear is also clipped on to a bandoleer

Hold A feature in the rock, such as a ledge, flake or crack, which provides a place to support the foot (foothold) or a place to grip with the hand (handhold)

Jam To wedge any part of the body into a crack to provide a hold. Hand-jams, finger-jams and fist-jams are particularly common techniques of using narrow cracks as useful holds

Jumar A make of ascender. Also used to describe actually climbing the rope by ascenders, as in 'He jumared up the rope'

Karabiner Often shortened to krab. A metal snap link with a spring-loaded gate in one side. It has numerous uses, the main one being as a connection between the rope and anchors

Krab *See* Karabiner

Layback A technique used to climb a corner crack where the hands grip and pull in one direction while the feet press the rock in the opposite direction

Leading The process by which the lead climber ascends a pitch first. The leader ascends placing protection while the second belays and holds the rope

Nut General name for a metal wedge or chock designed to provide an anchor by lodging into a constriction in a crack. Nuts come in a variety of sizes; larger nuts are threaded with rope and smaller ones with wire (when they are often called wires)

Offwidth A crack wider than the size of a fist but too narrow to admit the whole body. Generally awkward and strenuous to climb

PICTORIAL GLOSSARY

❶ The second climber belaying the lead climber i.e. holding his rope.

❷ She is anchored securely to the rock face by a nut and a bolt.

❸ A special belay device creates friction and effortlessly jams the rope if the leader falls.

❹ Using a tape sling dropped over a spike of rock for natural runner protection.

❺ This runner is a piton (or peg) which has been hammered into a crack. A karabiner (krab) links through the eye of the piton via a tape sling to another krab which the climber's rope runs through. The pitons can be removed, although they are sometimes left in for others to use. The tape sling holds the rope away from the rock face and therefore stops it dragging which could hinder progress.

❻ A pre-placed bolt runner (normally only found on 'sport climbs') provides protection when linked to the rope.

❼ Climber leading a pitch.

❽ Lead climber about to place a 'friend' (camming device) in a crack above him. This will also be linked to the rope, providing another piece of protection to safeguard a fall.

❾ Ledge (or stance) ideal for lead climber to stop and belay.

❿ When the leader arrives at the ledge, he will look for cracks and spikes to place anchors. When securely attached (belayed), he can then belay the rope for the second climber.

On Sight To lead a route without prior knowledge of the climb, the usual practice on traditional climbs. A better style of ascent than redpointing due to the adventurous nature of an on-sight ascent, where the climber has no knowledge of the holds above and the outcome can be much more uncertain

Peg Also known as a piton or pin. A metal spike designed to be hammered into a crack in the rock to provide an anchor. Pegs come in a range of shapes and sizes to fit a variety of widths of cracks

Pin *See* Peg

Pitch A section of a climb between consecutive belay stances. A pitch cannot be longer than the rope's length (usually 164 feet/50 m) and is usually much shorter to allow ease of communication between the leading and second climber. Short pitches also prevent drag on the rope, which can occur when the direction of the climb changes or goes around a corner or edge

Piton *See* Peg

Protection or Pro *See* Runners

Redpoint A method of ascent which involves practising the moves and the use of pre-placed protection (usually bolts) before the actual successful ascent. Frequently used in sport climbing and in style terms not as good as an on-sight ascent. *See also* Yo-yo and On Sight

Repeat To climb a route after it has had its first ascent

Runners Alternatively called running belay, protection, pro and gear. Runners are anchors placed by the lead climber which are then connected freely to the rope with a karabiner (and/or draw). If the lead climber falls, the rope going through the runner is held by the second belaying climber. This limits the fall to twice the distance the leader was above the runner. Runners are a crucial safety component for the climber

Seconding Climbing the pitch or climb second. The second climber belays and holds the rope while the leader climbs. The leader, on reaching the top of the pitch, stops and belays; the second then climbs, removing any runners that the leader may have placed. He or she is protected from above (apart from traverses) by the rope attached to the leader and therefore seconding is not as demanding as leading

Sling A loop of strong nylon tape or rope which can be used in a variety of ways. In particular a sling can be used as an anchor when placed over a spike of rock or threaded through a natural hole (or thread) in the rock

Sport Climb A climb pre-equipped with protection (usually bolts) and often climbed using redpoint style

Thread *See* Sling

Top-rope A rope dropped from the top of the climb or pitch, on routes with easy access to the top, before the climbers start the ascent. The climber then ascends, protected safely from above by the rope belayed by the climber's partner (as if seconding). Used to practise a climb or climb a route which the climbers do not or cannot lead

Traditional Climb Sometimes shortened to trad climb or adventure climbing. A climb using protection (such as slings, nuts and friends) placed on the lead. Normally climbed on sight

Traverse Moving horizontally left or right on a climb. It is as adventurous for the second climber as it is for the leader, as even when protection is placed on a traverse the rope usually does not protect the second from above

Yo-yo Where the leader has repeated attempts at a pitch, being lowered back to the ground or resting-point after each failed attempt. Not a very good style in which to climb a route but often necessary when attempting the hardest grades. Used in redpoint ascents

Further Reading

Bell, George, *Guide to the Cirque of the Unclimbables*, an invaluable guide available in complete form on the Internet at http://www.dtek.chalmers.se/Climbing/ Guidebooks/NorthAmerica/Unclimbables/index.html also see the 1996 Canadian Alpine Journal (vol. 79), where much of this guide was published

Bjørnstad, Eric, *Desert Rock*, Chockstone Press, 1996

Bonington, Chris (General Editor), *Great Climbs*, Mitchell Beazley, 1994

Burgess, Adrian and Alan, *The Burgess Book of Lies*, Cloudcap, 1994

Child, Greg, *Mixed Emotions*, The Mountaineers, 1993; *Thin Air*, Patrick Stephens, 1988

Cuthbertson, Dave; Duncan, Bob; Little, Graham; and Moody, Colin, *Climbers' Guide to Skye and the Hebrides* (vol. 2, *Rock and Ice Climbs*), Scottish Mountaineering Club, 1996

Fabian, Derek; Little, Graham; and Williams, Noel, *The Islands of Scotland including Skye*, Scottish Mountaineering Club, 1989

Fisher, Julian, *Cape Rock*, Nomad, 1996

Fyffe, Allen and Peter, Iain, *The Handbook of Climbing*, Pelham Books, 1990

Harrer, Heinrich, *The White Spider*, Flamingo, 1995

Howard, Tony, *Treks and Climbs in Wadi Rum, Jordan*, Cicerone Press, 1997

Knapp, Fred and Stevens, Michael, *Classic Desert Climbs*, 100 Select Guides, Boulder, 1996

Krakauer, Jon, *Into Thin Air*, Macmillan 1997

Lawrence ,T.E., *Seven Pillars of Wisdom*, Jonathan Cape, 1941

Roper, Steve and Steck, Allen, *Fifty Classic Climbs of North America*, Sierra Club Books, 1979

Simpson, Joe, all published by Jonathan Cape, *Dark Shadows Falling*, 1997; *Storms of Silence*, 1996; *The Water People*, 1992; *This Game of Ghosts*, 1993; *Touching the Void*, 1988

Index